ON THE WAY TO THE PULPIT

W. LEE TRUMAN

ON THE WAY TO THE PULPIT

iUniverse books may be ordered through booksellers or by contacting:

iUniverse
1663 Liberty Drive
Bloomington, IN 47403
www.iuniverse.com
844-349-9409

Because of the dynamic nature of the Internet, any web addresses or links contained in this book may have changed since publication and may no longer be valid. The views expressed in this work are solely those of the author and do not necessarily reflect the views of the publisher, and the publisher hereby disclaims any responsibility for them.

Any people depicted in stock imagery provided by Getty Images are models, and such images are being used for illustrative purposes only. Certain stock imagery © Getty Images.

ISBN: 978-1-6632-3058-4 (sc)
ISBN: 978-1-6632-3059-1 (e)

Library of Congress Control Number: 2022900947

Print information available on the last page.

iUniverse rev. date: 01/17/2022

DEDICATION

Dedicated to Louise who pushed me to put
words to my life story, and all the others
who insisted I write this book, and the over
five thousand of God's people my
wife and I have worked with.
Also to Mark, Rebecca, Timothy, and Nathan,
the most remarkable PKs.
But most importantly, I would like to dedicate this to
the love of my life, my one and only bride, my
Ruth, who has written and published nine books
and is the reason this writing is ever going to
see ink. Her know-how and patience in our lives
has been interwoven from the day we met.

CONTENTS

PART TWO

TRAVEL AND WORK WITH TEEN AGERS: A WINNING COMBINATION

MY FAITH STATEMENT

This is a personal word about the core of everything that is written on the pages of this book. It is a path of my life being led into the most exciting, rewarding and demanding job I could ever name, a life I tried to avoid and never wanted. Looking back, as what this book does, I now can clearly see the guidance of all that I am to where I was avoiding going. I was led to the pulpit, scared out of my wits to ever give a speech, let alone a sermon worth hearing, and do it every Sunday, which seems to come around every seven days.

Each time I came to a life decision, I internally knew what the right decision was. Now I can see the guidance of the hand of my Creator. There came a time early in my life when I asked myself: when I've come to the end of the line, what will I have wished I had given my life to? For me, I knew it was more than making money, though that had its deadened pull.

I compromised by preparing and being accepted as a missionary candidate. I met my incredible bride, Ruth, chose her, and she said yes to being my life partner. Because she was not of my denomination, I was dropped as an unacceptable missionary candidate. Or to put it more bluntly, I got the left foot of disfellowship, kicked out of my denomination because of choosing her as my soul's other half. And this was the best choice I ever made.

This story is about God taking the most unlikely mortal

and leading me into the life I have had. It has been His Grace and love with me, plus my Ruth all the way. This book is proof positive of what Jesus can do with very flawed clay.

Rev Lee

PROLOGUE

The life moments offered in this book are real. I know this for a fact because I lived them. I was named after my father until I was twelve years old, Guy Leroy Truman Jr., and I bore his name gladly and proudly. Dad was my hero but my Mom laid down my life path. She changed my name "Guy" to her family name "Wallace", a loser name on any school playground. I drew my first breath during the Great Depression. It was 1929 and I'm still breathing.

By the time I was twelve years old, I had 74 addresses, meaning I had little if any education. My Dad was in heavy construction and we went where the work was. At age twelve I was in a class of five 8th graders in Encino Elementary School, in Encino, California, which today is a city of almost 61,000 people.

At the time of writing this book, I am 92 and generally called 'Lee'. Those who knew me in my ministry would recall me as Rev Lee, which my car license plate announced and was the highest honor I ever attained or valued.

My wife Ruth and I now live in a retirement village in Camarillo, CA, and have celebrated 69 years of marriage, and I have an option for next year. We have four children: Mark, Becky, Tim, and Nathan, four lives God entrusted to our care. We have five grandchildren, Matthew, Christopher, John Patrick, Nick, and Mindy, who are as good as any I could ever hope for.

Read a little, read a lot. Enjoy it all. If not, just turn the page.

WELCOME TO THE MINISTRY

Night had just settled in this mountain community. There was nothing even resembling a street light and very few neighbors. We lived at the end of a dirt driveway at the top of a hill overlooking the valley. A soft knock at the door was a rare thing that caused both of us to stop to listen. This event called for caution.

Opening the door we found a terrified, disheveled, trembling teenager. We brought her in and she looked even worse in the light and obviously was badly abused. Her bruises bore wordless testimony to the story she had not yet told us. When she stammered her reason for coming to this refuge in the black of night, it got worse. She had just aborted in their outhouse, and her husband was in his "cups" threatening to kill her, and had the weapons to make good his threat. She summed it up with the words, "I'm terrified for my life." After sobbing, she told us where they lived. With no small concern, meaning scared, I left to go talk to her husband. I tried not to admit my fear to Ruth, or even admit what I was thinking to myself.

Locating their residence, it was black dark. I started to knock and the door suddenly opened with a 30-30 rifle pointing at my head. Whatever I stammered was met with "Shut the hell up." I was motioned to a stool with the no-argument end of the gun. In his drunken slurs, I was accused of taking his wife from him, and that was when he unchambered the gun, held the shell in the one bulb light, and rechambered the shell. This was followed with silence as he glared at me and again ordered me to "shut the hell up." A few more oaths along the same lines, while he clicked the safety on and off, left me silent. With no idea how much time had passed, I had not moved, while he paced the floor. He sat down and closed his eyes, I started to stand up, he waved the cannon he held; I sat back down.

Waiting till I was absolutely sure he had either passed out or was sleeping off his liquor, I tip-toed to the door and ran to my car. Such was the pastoral ministry in this mountain parish, our first church in California.

PART ONE

STARTING AT THE BEGINNING

✳ The Cat's Meow in High Volume

Try to understand my special feelings and respect I have for cats. I have no memory of any of this, since I had just learned to walk, and it had taken me over a year to do so. Or I may have been two years old? Mom never said. Where this happened, she never mentioned, but it was somewhere in the Mojave desert. It was on a dirt-moving construction site during the major depression which welcomed me into the world.

The cat's name was Tommy, a loving sleepyhead endowed with a cat's attitude of indifference. Mom said she heard Tommy over the noise of the dump trucks going by. Tommy was screeching up a storm, as Mom told it, but she was busy. After a bit, Mom checked to find out why all of the screeching cat noise.

Tommy was between me and my newfound playmate, a rattlesnake, who also seemed to want to either check me out or wanted to play drop dead. Tommy was doing all our pet cat could to keep us apart. I still have a place in my value system for cats.

FIRST MEMORIES

❋ Life In Yosemite Valley

My mother once casually mentioned that she broke the ice on the Merced River to wash my diapers, which meant we were living there in a tent in winter. It was worth noting what she had done for me. I never found Mom exaggerating anything. I am not sure I would ever do this for myself, but I heard her loud and clear. This may have been my first time living in this national park.

Pretending to pull levers like my dad, who was ready to dig the road to Glacier Point in Yosemite

Again, I have no memory because I was in diapers and not paying attention. We were there on a job or contract. My dad had to take a heavy piece of construction equipment, a steam shovel, into Yosemite valley. Only because of photos in my family photo album and my mother's comment is it notable. No doubt dad went head to head with the National Forest Rangers about the weight limits allowed on the road into the park.

The family photo shows the rig on the road, but this

piece of earthmoving equipment is stripped down to skeleton weight, having the ballast, boom, and all of that which makes it a digging machine, removed.

❋ What You Were Never Told About Yosemite Valley

The second time living there was in a year-round wood-framed cabin with a canvas roof, wood stove, and used dynamite boxes for furniture. Remember this was the time of the great depression. The job was to build an all-weather road to Glacier Point to serve the Glacier Point Hotel. The road in use then closed in November because of snow.

Home sweet home, but hard to heat

The staff at the hotel started the Firefall tradition. Later the crowds became overwhelming to see this well remembered, unique spectacle. Finally, the Park Rangers said no more Firefall.

This next bit I have never heard a Ranger mention in any story told about the Valley history or even when asked about it. None so far has had any clue to what I am talking about, but I have very real memories of this happening.

The work crew used a great deal of dynamite to blast the way for the new road up to Glacier Point and the Firefall was done privately by the hotel staff.

Before the Firefall fell, the road workmen would tie several sticks of Hercules dynamite onto a rope, drop it over the edge of Glacier Point, and we in the valley would, out loud, count the number of echoes as the blast would bounce back and around the valley. No doubt it was the length of the rope that determined how many times the blast sound echoed and re-echoed.

Now you know a bit of history of one of our most famous features in California, that is not acknowledged by any authority of the Valley's history, because it was done by creative working stiffs, all private citizens with a touch of the crazies.

✳ Tumbleweed Christmas

It took me a long time to be aware that Christmas for my family was different than for most who understand and celebrate this special day. I became savvy as to how special a day it was, when we were living in the high desert. Almost everything that was ordered for Christmas morning came from the Sears and Roebuck catalog.

Sears seemed to offer everything except the Christmas tree. Our tree was a windblown tumbleweed. Good choice and careful pruning were all that was needed. Decorations were another matter. Mom put us to work cutting strips of colored paper. My sister and I would then turn them into a Christmas chain with a paste made from flour and water. The colorful chain would be wound onto the "tree" and the house would be filled with Christmas cheer and laughter.

Next would be popcorn sewn onto one of Pop's fishing

lines. This I never came close to mastering, but it all went on the tree. Mom would take a ribbon and make a few bows, and the tree I saw was in all of its glory. As for me, these were the best Christmas trees ever.

Of course we all would stand back and admire our creation. With the night sky flecked with stars just for me, it all was as good as it could get. We tried to make a snowman for the outdoors, but the tumbleweed remembered its nature and soon tumbled on, playing with the wind.

My dad's work was in the Mojave Desert, so he worked one of two six hour night shifts instead of days, because of the wilting heat during the day. Also it was six hour work to allow more men to have a job during the big depression. When he got off work at dawn, he always had a good word about our tree efforts before he went to bed.

Dad knew when Christmas was arriving by the Orion constellation coming over the horizon, which soon was close enough to reach up and touch. It quickly became prominent in the night panorama of stars. And when Orion made its appearance, I was told Christmas was soon to be. Mom would pack the 1932 Buick with a bed made up in the back. Sis and I would go to sleep in the back seat and knew when we woke up, we would be well on our way to either Grandma Wallace in Phoenix or Grandma Truman in LA.

Having helped Mom load the car, I knew every item packed, right down to the water bags hanging from the front bumper. There was a purpose in this, as I had school mates that doubted there was a Santa. I did not know what was true.

I made sure that my parents had overheard me ask Santa for a particular red wagon with balloon tires. It was top of the line and no such wagon was packed into the Buick. The answer to the question of there being a Santa or no Santa, was on the table. I was going to find out.

When I woke up early at Grandma Wallace's home in Phoenix, I crept into the front room, and there was the red wagon with balloon tires under their strange-looking Christmas tree. I became a believer. I kept that wagon until we moved from Colville, Washington (1956). When we left, we had a jumble sale. A friend priced the wagon, then bought it.

Years later I asked Pop how did that happen? He said he called Loy, my uncle, who lived in Phoenix, and asked him to buy the wagon, which he did. That, once and for all, settled the question, "Is there a Santa?" The answer is: "Yes, there is," and his name is Uncle Loy, but Dad was the elf.

Family gathering at grandparents

✳ A Big Thanksgiving

It happened every year.

Not sure if it had anything to do with faith, but it sure took place at my grandparents Truman's home every year. There were times we would arrive early and I got to help with the "big chore," right along beside my older cousins.

This was getting down the 2" x 12" x 12' boards from the garage attic. They were right where we put them last year at this time of the season.

These boards, with a number of saw horses, became the benches. Then came more boards which became tables, and together they made one long table, often which stretched from the front of the living room through the dining room and out into the kitchen, and some years beyond into the back porch.

For myself, seeing a fireplace was special enough, but add this with all the side tables to hold the food brought each time Gram's door opened, was pure excitement. My Mom cooked over a gasoline stove with a fold up oven…

Each branch of the family added their weight of goodies to the sagging tables. This may be a bit overstated but to me, it was an awesome wide-eyed truth. I think that the wives tried to outdo each other with their dishes, but it was the pies and baking that got my attention. The real goodies were set apart on one whole table and they were at nose level tempting for me.

You see, there were eight children in my father's family, and with spouses and their progeny, it made a reasonably sized crowd. In the mandatory photo always taken after this gathering for one such feast, I counted 87 in that photo who had come together for this event. By now some of you are thinking I may be referring to Thanksgiving? Yes, it was the same date as the whole nation observed on this national holiday, but no prayers were said at our gathering, at least not out loud.

I really had not understood then why there were no bowed heads or words of thanks offered. The reason was that we were a blended religious family. For example, my cousin and buddy saved some of his home dinner which he slipped into my hand, asking if this tasted like meat? His family ate no "flesh" as an act of faith. One other thing was that they never picked up their newspaper off the lawn on Saturday because the day was holy for them. They lived two blocks down the street from my grandparents.

One part of the family was Greek Orthodox. My uncle Lou had emigrated to this country and married my aunt Edna, my father's sister. Their first-born son was named George Louis Zavas. This rotation of the middle and first names had been going on for four hundred years in Greece. They lived just down the street.

Another branch of the family was atheist and hardcore agnostic and not until much later did I know how committed they were in their belief system. Yet another branch on the family-tree was Christian Science. Uncle "Mac" was a straight arrow and lived his faith as did his family, except for one cousin a bit older than me, who gave bad a bad name and his sister is my lifelong friend.

Me? I had no idea what I, or my family, was. Mom always started a Sunday School wherever we lived. My mother's father was a Mormon who passed away when I was five months old. I can see now why no prayers were ever said. We were a mixed up family, somewhat like a dog's breakfast.

What I once overheard in my uncles' conversation, did shake up my world. Seems there was an uncle I never met because when he was a young man he was killed in a construction accident. Uncle Kenny was employed digging a tunnel, and oxygen was brought into the tunnel via a rubber hose laid out on the tunnel floor. What I overheard was that an older brother, thinking in terms of a practical joke, turned up the pressure so the hose would whip around creating a dust storm in the tunnel. Either someone was smoking or lit a match so they could see, but all workers in that tunnel died in a flaming hell.

It was the bottom of the great depression and I overheard harsh words said as to who would pay for Uncle Kenny's grave marker. My dad finally picked up this expense.

There was another uncle I never met. The story goes that he joined the Navy and had a dispute with an officer. He settled it by taking a whack at the officer's chin. This being a rather bad no-no according to Navy regs, my uncle changed his name and hid under his new name the rest of his life. He lies beneath a headstone with his chosen new name, and is buried beside my great grandfather in the midst of the family plot in Inglewood, California.

Mostly I played with my cousins I only saw about once a year. But I also tried to sample each pie and cake on this wondrous day of feasting. I never was able to accomplish this goal, but there was always next year.

❋ Fire in the Camp

Temporary housing for the construction crew was pressed together in a line. Next to our place, a neighbor boy was asked by his dad to fill the coal-oil tank to heat the water for his bath. The stove was burning and the new fuel created an explosion which started a roaring fire, and our place was quickly engulfed. With incredible luck, the boy was more scared than hurt. My dad yelled ``FIRE" and threw the red glass balls, labeled "In Case Of Fire," which turned out to be a joke. Dad and Mom grabbed us two kids and ran out of the tinder box housing.

Mom, no doubt in a state of panic, then ran back into the house. It was fast filling with smoke. She went to the closet, took down her never worn new Easter coat, removed dad's paycheck out of the pocket, hung her new coat back up and ran, making her escape again, now waving dad's paycheck.

By this time the whole camp had gathered to do what they could. One man stood at the kitchen window tossing Mom's good china out the window with a baseball player's effort throwing to first base.

My part of shame in all of this was that I had put my playing blocks in my sister's bed, and a neighbor, seeing the lump in her bed, tried to rescue her with blinding smoke and the fire nipping at his heels.

Dad's mechanic tools were stored under the house and the fire took all of the temper out of them, so I inherited my first set of Black Hawk tools which were useless, but which I have kept always as a reminder of our house burning in the desert. I have put the temper back in the ones most often used.

Dad found a windowless storage shed sitting in the midst of a field of eggplant. It was unharvested because of the depressed cost of shipping. From that shed, Pop took two trailer loads of trash to the dump. Then we had a home again and all the eggplant we could eat.

✳ USS Arizona

It was my Mom who gave me a lifetime memory in 1937 when the newspaper announced the invitation to come aboard The USS Arizona. "Pride of the US Navy", one of two "Super Dreadnoughts" boasting twelve huge 14" guns and twenty-two 5" guns, it was the best we had. (On Dec 7th, 1941, Pearl Harbor was bombed and 1,177 sailors and Marines were killed on this ship. 335 sailors survived, mostly because they were on shore leave). I was super excited as we got on the launch to take us out to board this mighty Navy ship, that obviously commanded the seven seas. Then it happened.

Mom, getting off the shore launch, slipped on the gangplank and fell, ripping a wound the length of her left lower leg. The ship's medical sailors immediately took her below deck to the ship's hospital, where she was for the whole day.

This left me free to explore this wonder of all there was to investigate. I had the eager help of the sailors who had not made liberty. Everything had obviously been inspected, polished twice, and all was in first-rate shipshape. And this included the uniforms of every sailor down to their shoes. Crew members were showing adults the tour, but I had the run of the ship and a number of "shipmates", who were at loose ends and wanted to show me their specialty on the ship. The one place I liked the best was the Geedunk shop that had endless kinds of ice cream, etc, and it was all free. I quickly learned that if I said "please," I got a double-dip.

I was wide-eyed to see inside the turrets where I saw how they loaded these 14" monster guns. I stood on the Bridge, and the helm which turned easily, was taller than I was. I also found where they kept the maps and flags. The steam engine was massive and I could not put my arms around the propeller shaft. I got to see the radio room where they were sending code to some far off place. I was surprised to see the print shop where they put out a dally paper. A lot else I have forgotten, but not the sailors who loved their ship and told me tales that left me wide-eyed and wanting to grow up to be like them.

Years later, as I read the names on the Pearl Harbor Memorial Wall of those who had died, Dec. 7th, Sunday, 1941, I wondered which sailors took care of me and gave me a life memory I cannot forget. Kneeling before that wall I prayed - but also mostly smiled - remembering the best gift I ever received from strangers who all wore Navy uniforms while showing off the USS Arizona to a wide eyed kid, me.

✳ Bartending

It was a Labor Day celebration unlike any other. It began with an all-night drive from dad's job site in order to get to the Labor Day celebration. It was mostly a parade through downtown Los Angeles, with the crowd lining both sides of the street. With flags flying, bands playing and massive numbers of people. Local 12 of the International Union Of Operating Engineers was one of the marching participants. My dad was one of the original organizers of this Union. Excited, I stood with the admiring crowd, but when dad came by, I ran and joined the parade, marching in step with my dad. I had grown up body-wise, but was still young enough to be thoughtlessly impulsive to a fault, something I am still dealing with.

The next item on that day's doings was to go to a brewery in downtown LA. It had a large hall with a live band, and most of those union members who showed up attempted to dance, but a lot of toes were stepped on. The big draw, as I saw it, was the unlimited free beer, but only one bartender and a long line of those who were thirsty waiting. I helped him until he got tipsy. He left or joined the gents out on the floor. I mean the ones not dancing but were flat on their back. I hustled really hard as did a lot of other underagers who helped deliver the suds, but I saw no fun in being blotto.

I remember one man who had a bartowel tied to his left wrist and over his neck, then with the other hand, he could hoist his beer and not spill a drop. Another man was on the floor but could still drink his beer. What was in it for me? The going rate for a tip was a nickel and I was in tall cotton with my newfound means of pocketing money. Greed knows no age limit.

No, I did not take a sip of this strange beverage because my mother had said "NO," with that word spoken meaning no further discussion. It was a Labor Day I have no problem recalling, as I crossed off the possible future vocation list of "bartender." This was even if I did have two pockets heavy with nickels and I made the change for paper money and kept moving as fast as I could to meet the demand. I never did tell Mom how much I made in tips, but I knew what it was like to be really rich.

✳ Excitement at Ten

The one and only time I went deer hunting with my dad and what makes it come to mind: It was in the hills of San Luis Obispo where Pop was digging the cut for a new highway section of the 101. First, we came across an abandoned mine, which had dynamite sticks scattered all around the grounds. As I stooped to pick one up, Dad yelled, "DON'T TOUCH IT! You can't tell how unstable it may be." We left that place and moved on. This in itself is a bit unnerving as I well knew, but it was the information of the adult world and I obeyed without question.

The next unforgettable item happened in the deep brush when a rifle shot ripped the air and we both heard the zing as it tore through the brush. Dad slammed me to the ground, then he dropped to one knee, and emptied the Winchester 25-35 magazine in one burst at the sky. I never knew a lever action saddle gun could be fired that fast. His comment was that the shooter had seen or heard the brush move, and the hunter might have taken a second shot of us moving, thinking we were deer.

My Dad later said, "I'll bet that was the first time a deer ever shot back." We never saw a deer and to my knowledge, my dad never went deer hunting again. If he did, he didn't take me.

Living the elite life with a home on wheels

❋ The Road Home

There are a few events in growing up that are embedded deeply in all of us. It is in the events, guidance, love or status that make up our young lives, that shape our thinking or perception. This event changed my life.

A quick setting of the scene. My folks had saved enough to buy the largest house trailer made by and named "Road Home." It was an 18 1/2 footer and was the wonder of our new home on wheels. Dad said, while showing it off, "Your shirt is always in the same drawer." This was no small thing after living in a tent or whatever. Besides this, it was the biggest trailer they made and we got a four place set of dishes with the trailer. They were four different colors. I chose yellow and from then on my meals always came on yellow china. We were always parked in the most prominent spot, as a way of showcasing the state of available trailers.

Our new home had two benches in the front and a table in between where we ate together in our "dining room." My sister slept on one bench under which was a very small bathtub, never used. I slept on the other bench, under which was storage. It seemed that I grew and my feet were soon hanging over the end of my bench bed. Something had to be done. Dad made three pallets that fit in the back of his pickup which, when put on the ground, formed a porch for my new bedroom floor. It could always move with us.

Wrapping canvas around two of three awning poles, I had an outside private bedroom and it was all for myself, well almost. A young pup had joined the family. He kept my feet warm at night. This worked fine until winter got serious and my faithless dog opted to scratch at the door of the warm trailer to be let in, leaving me to keep my own feet warm. And I had named this traitor pooch, "Buddy."

For personal protection at night, I had an automatic .45 caliber cap pistol with a full roll of caps. Having just seen the motion picture with Bob Hope, "The Cat and the Canary," where Bob Hope was in bed, and hands kept coming out of the opening headboard to choke him, I armed up. This cap pistol was under my pillow and my Red Ryder BB gun was within reach. I also had a priceless item. It was a blanket that had been made by my grandmother Wallace. It was pure warmth and a grandmother's love in every stitch. That, and Mom always left the porch light on for me.

The trailer park had a recreation hall, and a two-sided central shower with bathrooms for the whole park. It also had one other thing never mentioned: you had no doubt which way the wind was blowing, because across the road was a dairy farm.

A creek ran past the park on the west side with a deep channel. It was dry most of the year. Several friends and I tunneled into the creek bank, making a room at the end big enough for all of us. A sign was posted. "No Girls Allowed." That afternoon, returning home from school, I found that the whole thing had collapsed and even the sign was covered up. None of us ever mentioned this, or dug another "club-house". We had sworn secrecy. All of this my parents never knew, but I saw this could have been the end of me.

All was going along just dandy except for my fickle dog. There was one Christmas tree for the whole camp and it was in the Common Hall. My guess is that dad had rented the hall for Xmas. It was obvious the place where "Santa" would leave anything we had whispered in his ear, or mentioned to Mom or Dad. I was not a believer. I was a wise ten years old and at this age, one is careful not to upset a good thing.

Now, one problem. With Christmas Eve there was always a problem of going to sleep. There was the rather faint hope that Santa knew where we lived, and would leave the pony wished for with every candle blown out on every birthday cake, and tacked onto every Christmas wish list. The problem was that somehow the park hall was locked. How did I know?

Waking up way too early in my personal bedroom, I, in my pajamas, and in the dark, tried the locked recreation door. I then looked through every window and could not make out much. Much later the camp manager came and unlocked the door, turned on the lights, and I was in, and then it was the fury of torn Christmas paper in the air with no restraint.

There, under the Christmas tree, was a Lionel train with four cars, in all of its model railroad glory. I plugged in the transformer and the train was off on a life of its own. It would never be better than this and I reveled in it all.

In my Christmas stocking, hung on the back of a chair, there was a pocket knife. Why do I remember this knife? To this day I do not understand what moved me to stick it into an electoral outlet and notch the big blade.

Christmas was wonderful and it was 365 days till Christmas again. A thought occurred to me for the first time, "Where would I keep a pony?" All of this had its beginning from my reading the book, "Smoky, The Cow Horse." Life went on, pony-less, but railroading now took center billing without looking back.

At this moment the sun made its debut and my sister and mom came through the door, fully dressed, and just in time to notice that I had plugged in a lead melting pot to make my own miniature soldiers, and its three legs had burned three holes in the main room rug. One more thing that Pop must have paid for.

Moving on up to real luxury, indoor plumbing and two bedrooms

✳ A House at Last!

The first house we owned was built in the middle of an empty hayfield in the San Fernando Valley. This was located where the 405 and 101 freeways in Southern California now cross, so everyone drives through the area which had been my sister's (Guyvanna's) bedroom. Lots of memories in the second lane of the freeway going from the 101 to the 405.

Celebrating living in our own house was a new experience for our family. Watching it being built was something special, as we were living in the house trailer. (I was still checking to see if a strange car had a hitch and was one of us.)

During our first weeks living in this new area, a kid on a bike stopped and invited me to CE (Christian Endeavor), with me impressed by the rabbit skin on his bike seat. He also told me with a smile that there would be girls there. That didn't stop me; I went anyway.

I became lifelong friends with Bill Cooper that day to the end of his days. I still miss him. One time I stayed over at his house as a teen after a late double date. His mother called out from her bedroom in the dark, "Bill, You been out gum suckin' again?"

How do you answer that?

✳ Poor Impy

This is a confession of cat abuse. My parents had never had their own house before, and now on a dirt street in Sherman Oaks, they were having one built and it was with all the frills of a two-bedroom mansion. My sister got the second bedroom. My room was built behind the garage by my dad and grandfather for me.

Two goodies I remember them showing off to friends was a lock on the bathroom door that could be unlocked from the outside.The other one was a milk door some four feet up an outside wall. It was this built-in item by the back steps where our milkman could leave milk. He still left it on the back porch, never once in the milk box. The milk chute also opened inside the service porch. This item, also, was never used. It had an inside door that could be locked. Both doors were always left open.

Our pet cat, Impy, recognized this as a cat door and began using it to go in and out. Impy would jump from the tree in the back yard and hit this rather small hole in the house wall. This pet had flying speed with accurate aim in order to do this. Instead of appreciating what the cat was doing, I closed the inside door of this milk chute. The cat flew, hit the hole, and met in less than a foot, a steel door that was closed. Our cat never tried this again.

As a preteen I thought it was funny, now I apologize. I do recall that I felt I owed a debt to my pet cat Tommy, but -- Impy was a very strange cat.

❋ The Swimming Pool

High on the list of "must-haves" for most pre-teens, is a swimming pool. Living in rural Sherman Oaks, such luxury did not exist. Asking my Dad a question while he was reading the newspaper, knowing that timing is everything when really big issues are approached, the question was: "May I dig a swimming pool in the backyard"?

Hearing only an unidentifiable sound in response, I morphed it in my head into an enthusiastic "YES." The pool in my thoughts was to be in operational use that week. Having been on many job sites, I knew surveyor stakes. First, it was staked out as ideal. It was quickly obvious even to me that I had it way too big. Besides I would have had to take out two rows of the orange trees in the orchard. Several prudent reductions later, I had the right compromise.

Starting at the shallow end with a pick and shovel and my wagon to haul away what I excavated, I knew within the hour this was not going to work. I needed help. I called on my good friend Stanley up the street and told him if he wanted to swim, he had to help. We were on an eight party line with a lot of folks who listened to every call. We both made calls and kids of all ages signed on.

Some lived quite a distance away, and some I did not know, but none had access to the swimming pool if they didn't come and move dirt. All knew the opportunity it promised. They all bent to the task with a will and intense purpose, with an eye to future use.

The indentation in our back yard quickly grew as the dirt flew. A little organizing and we were moving dirt at a good rate. The excavated earth was taken to the orange orchard and spread out by those who brought wagons. Pick and shovel crew rotated and we soon had an impressive hole in the ground. And dust in the air.

Then Dad came home from work. I really didn't know how to read faces but there was no doubt what his face said. He had to have taken a deep breath and brought everything to a screeching halt. He bought off my crew by offering to pay all their way to the movie theater, and I recall this was with popcorn. My joy got to be filling up this dry crater in the backyard without any help.

❋ Pistols and Blue Jays

I bought a very cheap pistol advertised in an ad on the back of a comic book. I was in the 8th grade, and of course, took it to school. A friend liked it and said he could bore it out to a larger size and he knew where we could get bullets that would be just right. As I recall, its caliber was smaller than a 22. Taking it home, I tried to show it to my dad but he was more interested in the morning newspaper. I am sure he didn't hear me. No problem.

I went to the wood garage door and in the dust drew a circle. Standing just outside the kitchen window where dad was having breakfast, I drew aim and fired at the circle. I think the shot hit the garage door at the same time my dad hit the back door. I never saw that gun again till I was in college. I have it now, and it does look like a cheap toy. I have all of my fingers and no urge to ever fire it again.

Our family doctor sealed any interest I had in that gun as he quietly informed me, "Tell me when you are going to shoot it again and I will prepare to save as much of your hand as I am able." I suspect that my Mom put him up to telling me this. They both said it in an off-handed way.

We raised chickens and rabbits. This meant morning and evening chores, feeding, cleaning cages, and all that had to be done daily. I had an egg route and also 16 cages of rabbits in the rabbit house. Dad liked rabbits and we ate or sold rabbits, but always salted away the rabbit skins and when the trunk was full, sold them.

The biggest problem was that birds called Blue-Jays (I was told they were "butcher birds") would peck holes in the eggs in the chicken nests. My thing was to put some eggs in a bucket, set it out and wait. I sat on the back porch with my 22 Savage rifle and when they perched on the bucket edge to check out the eggs, I shortened their life span. Never had a complaint from the birds or the house on the next street just built. I seriously doubt any kid could do that now and stay out of jail, but it upped the number of eggs I could sell.

Our family custom was to celebrate the week on Saturday evening with tacos and homemade ice cream. Guess who got to have the honor of turning that ice cream crank? The honor part wore off quite quickly, so innovation looked for an easier way and it took over.

My dad, while working in the desert, had adapted an old Nash to get across the desert to the job. When we left that job he traded it for a heavy duty construction drill. It was geared way down to slow. When I took off the handle from the ice cream freezer and chucked the freezer handle shaft into the drill, it worked better than I had hoped. The serendipity was that when the ice cream was frozen, the drill didn't slow down. The ice cream bucket just made 360' circles in the air until I turned off the drill. There was no doubt that the ice cream was frozen.

I would rather have had a pony. Now I
know how very special she was.

❋ Younger Sisters are the Crabgrass in the Lawn of Life

This comes under the heading then and now as scary dumb. I almost killed my sister. Chemistry class at school had us growing copper crystals, and I wanted to also do this at home. So I set up this experiment in the garage and was growing copper crystals big time. I had filled all available bottles with the copper sulfate, but needed one more container. I had an empty soft drink bottle and used it to hold the last of the copper sulfate mix.

My little sis, seeing a full bottle of soda in the garage and thinking it was mine, took a huge gulp. She had to go to the hospital and have her stomach pumped. I was a big bad brother, but grateful even today that she came home alive, even if she told the story to everyone she knew or would listen to what I had done. I dared not defend myself as every adult was shocked at what I had set up (which was nothing but a chemistry experiment). I was one dangerous, evil, big brother.

No one ever mentioned that my sister was stealing some of what she thought was my drink.

❋ Riding the Raft

One winter in rural Sherman Oaks, Ca., my best friend and I went to see the full Los Angeles river running bank to bank strong. it was a rare, strange sight. Standing looking at this body of rushing water one of us suggested we make a raft, and so we did. Riding our scrap wood water vehicle we were with Tom Sawyer and Huck Finn on a high adventure, riding the rough waves of the Mississippi.

Passing Van Nuys was a wake-up call. We were moving

pretty fast, but having great fun as we bounced along, when we both realized it would be a really long walk back. Disembarking our watercraft was harder to do than we thought and we were a good way beyond anything that looked familiar. We abandoned our raft and were right, it was a long walk back. Mom said, "YOU WHAT?"

The school was flooded out and we were bored. In a large weed field, we started to dig an underground clubhouse. First an entry hole just small enough not to be noticed, and a short tunnel to the club room that would serve as our private boys only club space. (Girls had cooties.) Realizing the roof on such a big room, in this soil, would never stay in place, we used scrap wood for the ceiling. Covering it with sod, the problem was solved.

Walking home from school, I saw this pipe sticking up out of the ground where our clubhouse was. The owner of the lot had hired a tractor to plow his land. The tractor fit exactly in our club room but out of sight. It's exhaust pipe stood in the center of our main room. I could only guess at the words used when this all happened. When questioned I simply answered, "What lot?" A phrase used only once, then I caved in and owned up.

I think my dad paid for digging out that tractor.

✳ Confession

This took place in my seventh and eighth-grade year. I was rolling out of bed at 4:30 am. in order to pick up my newspapers at 5:00 a.m. to deliver on my paper route. There were two of us covering all of Sherman Oaks. The skill was to fold the paper in such a way that it would not fly apart when thrown. The war had just started and there were no rubber bands to be had at any price.

The downside of this was collecting a dollar and a half every month from never-at-home subscribers. Next was rain and there was only wax paper to keep the newspaper dry which it didn't. When it was raining, most of the streets were mud, which meant pushing the bike, not riding. Because Sunday's paper was so heavy, I walked or pushed my balloon tire bike the whole route.

Then came the big issue: the papers were late, or very late, being delivered to us. Subscribers called the paper asking or yelling, "Where is my paper?" When I finished I rode my bike to school, which started at eight, and there were only five of us in our grade, so being late was hard to not be noticed.

The other carrier and I would check an abandoned gas station to see if the papers happened to have been dropped off there. One morning we found the station was unlocked. We entered but nothing there was worth taking in our value system, but it was a seed planted.

We found a nursery facing Ventura Boulevard easy to get into, since I had worked there. I took a handful of seed packs and then did not know what to do with them. My cohort in crime found he could sell almost anything at his school, but he also figured out how to open the cash registers.

The Police picked him up at school. Then it was my turn when I got off the school bus and was walking home, which set off the neighborhood gossip on the eight party line. She cast word feathers to the wind that I knew could never all be picked up.

This walk home and seeing a police car waiting, was a terrifying moment like no other. The result? In a flash, I was scared straight. It was my mother's tears that said it all. I was put on probation by the court for a year and no more paper route. Dad never said a word but I knew he was disappointed beyond words by my acts. I was ashamed of myself.

My dad"s worst punishment were his using the dreaded words to tell me that I knew better. He knew that Mom had taken me to Sunday School and church every Sunday and how could I be a thief? I would rather have gladly taken a hundred belt lashes instead of hearing those words.

Now you know why this was never told to anyone, especially our kids and my wife, until now.

※ Jink's Lake

It was the height of summer joy and we were on our way. I rode in the back of my dad's pickup with a squirming gathering of my cousins, singing, yelling as loud as we could and no one saying, "keep the noise down."

Even the back road up to Big Bear was special because my dad had dug it out of the mountain when I was a baby. How did I have this in mind? Mom had pictures of me in a high chair made out of dynamite boxes. She had me out of the tent and behind a tree because they were blasting not far away. Every curve in that mountain road was and is special to me.

Los Angeles was hot in the summer, so my grandmother and my aunt Edna set up a small kingdom at Barton Flats Campground. Summer's high point was to go there and stay as long as possible. Each of us grandchildren had an assignment and mine was to gather pine needles, and anything else asked of me. The pine needles were to be put under the bedrolls. From sunup till the last embers of the campfire flickered out, it was pure special fun.

If we had our chores done, we were free to go on a hike up to Jink's Lake, which was all of us, ASAP. The reward was swimming in the icy water, dunking, splashing, and all of the laughter and noise we could make. An older cousin broke the lock on a canoe chain and paddled away like King Neptune. Not sure if I saw it as stealing but I was jealous.

It was in the bathhouse that what happened caused me to avoid him as much as I could. I had stretched my swim time as long as possible. He was in the changing room with me and he was looking through a hole he had cut in the wall. I knew that the other side was the girl's side.

I also knew that my girl cousin was changing in the next room. No, I did not call out. I just avoided him after this for the rest of his troubled life.

II

THE DANGEROUS TEEN YEARS

✳ High School Misdeeds

Bussing began for me the first day of school from Sherman Oaks to Canoga Park, some 18 miles. There were two of us guys on the bus at the first stop. Me, being a "snotty nosed" freshman and the other rider, Phil, who never said a word to me. He was a senior who was President of the Student Body. Now I know he was concerned about what the future would be for him. It was 1941. He was killed as a Marine during the invasion of Guadalcanal, which made WWII very real for me.

When the bus arrived at Canoga Park HS, the bell rang. Everyone came to attention, no matter where they were. All stopped to face the flag pole. The trumpet sounded and the flag was raised, a job I did for some two years and was proud to have done so.

I remember I had two questions on my first day in physics class. One I never asked: "How can a mirror have two different reflections at the same time?" The second was, "How can I be in the back of my dad's pickup and moving, and then toss a ball in the air, and have the ball move along with me and I catch it." One word answer, "inertia."

It was in chemistry that I was excited, supplemented with the metal shop. Rockets were the wonder weapon of the time and I could turn a rocket body in the metal shop and make the propellant in chemistry. All resulted in a 100% spectacular failure rate.

We were also blowing glass to make our own usable chemical experiment items and vessels. By blowing a glass bubble and leaving a stem, and then filling the bubble with water, I could then seal the stem. If this was held over the bunsen burner there would be a blast off. The steam then moved it so fast across the lab I was never able to time it. Thus was my steam-driven rocket. All was well until I was asked what I was doing. Afterward, Gail Austin showed me her bleeding leg; the shattered glass had done its thing. I blessed her then and now for not saying a word, just going to the nurse for a patch up.

The one that did receive the attention of the Principal, was because the school had received some used submarine batteries. The scuttlebutt was that they had been taken from a Japanese sub. Now I doubt it, but they were huge and may have been sub batteries. With these and a big coil, the resulting electric spark was delightfully blue and long. I hooked it up to the lockers outside of the physics lab.

Those students returning from lunch had a "shocking experience" as they tried to open their lockers. Those who experienced this "re-volting" experience joined me on the other side of the hall to watch the next "victim." It was good fun till faced with the rather upset, red faced principal. He mumbled of possible police involvement and the word "expulsion" being in about every third sentence he tossed about, mostly, as I recall, through clenched teeth. We agreed no more on my part....or else.

I believed him!

※ The Furball Car

Turning 14, my growth hormones welcomed and embraced me big time. My goal was to get behind any steering wheel, ASAP. Solving this my way was to not ask. I started backing out dad's pickup, turning it around, and then backing it so it faced the street. This made it an easy exit for my dad. He never objected and I had time behind the wheel.

I moved up a peg when I got under the hood of the family car. It was a 1938 Century Buick, painted forest green. While changing the oil in this car, I spilled some on the fender. Wiping it off, the paint looked brand new or even better. Marveling at this easy method of polishing to look like a new paint job, I undertook the task of wiping down the whole car with oil. It sparkled and I grinned. I couldn't wait till dad saw what I had discovered. I was never going to wax any car again.

Remember we lived on a dirt street in Sherman Oaks. Dad came home in his pickup, jumped out, stared for a moment at the gleaming Buick, got in, and drove away. When he returned the Buick looked like a big fat furball. Dad never said a word. He didn't have to. You have no clue how long it took with soap, hot water, and hand buffing car wax to undo what was so quickly done.

The fallout from this was that my dad borrowed a motor patrol (grader) and began simi-paving the whole block. Coming home from school I was somewhat surprised to find that almost every vehicle that the city of Van Nuys owned was on our street. The issue was that there had to be a law somewhere that you are not allowed to pave your own street.

I no longer had the chore of using the garden hose to lay the dust of the street. Pop had settled the dust problem and the rest was settled in court.

It was good to have someone else in the family in trouble for a change.

My pride and joy, but no money for a windshield

✳ Ford Enters My Life

Any after-school program, including sports (football, track) meant missing the bus and then hitchhiking home, which wasn't all that bad. Gas rationing meant a lot of us were doing what was called riding our thumbs. With an armload of books, most good citizens would give me a lift. This included a Carmelite monk who invited me to his study for lessons. I read more than he recommended. I asked a lot of questions -- and he discontinued the study.

This holding out my thumb all changed when I asked my dad when I could have a car. He responded, "When you can pay for it."

I had been burying my earned money in fruit jars in the backyard using a posthole digger. Digging them all up to make a withdrawal was a ditch digging problem. The bills in one jar were wet and moldy, which the seller reluctantly accepted. I now owned a '31 Model A Ford five window business coupe. It was parked in the driveway when Pop came home the next evening. He never said a word. This happily ended riding my thumb.

My new motive for attending Sunday School was that the teacher's husband had two Indy cars. They were Novi Specials, inline, straight 8 cylinders, in competition at the Indianapolis 500. They were fast, beautiful, but never finished the race because something always broke. There was an Offenhauser shop close by, producing the winning cars. I often visited there, and set my next goal to bring forth the fastest car in the San Fernando Valley, which in my inner world, I thought I did.

The police had flathead Fords with one Holly 97 carburetor. Most anything I did to get more horsepower worked, so outrunning a police car was the norm. This was not true of motorcycle cops. For the most part there was a working peace with the police.

They let us car guys block the newly built freeway which was by the Van Norman Reservoir. It was safe, since there were no side streets. Here we could run our heats on Wednesday night. My education slowed down, and violin lessons ended. I didn't run with the cubic dollar cars, but I held my own. The paint job was out of a spray can, but under what my mom called "the bonnet," I had the good stuff that really turned the rear wheels quick.

As with most who are high school alumni, this is only a smidgen of what happened during those years, especially the ones misspent or that caused the Principal to greet me with no smile. I tended to get into fights. I did know how to fight to win, which is to just never give up. I had learned through the years, being tested at every school attended, by every bully who had to try out the new kid, me.

Then I went forward at a Youth For Christ rally calling for those who wanted to accept Jesus into their inner temple, life and guidance. I knew I was out of step in my life. That night I made a choice to be a Christian. Someone prayed with me. This was life changing-serious, and it was.

Everything had changed, or as the scripture says, "all things were made new," and I found that it was me. Mom had always started a Sunday School at every job site where we landed. Like it or not, I was kept in Sunday School and maybe church, if there was one, and it all now paid off for me. I realized I could no longer cheat in class on tests, and I was a practicing pro. Sliding by was easy because I could cheat.

Now I had to study which was a new experience for me. It was hard and there was little attraction to hit the books, and this was kept near the bottom of things to do. Now it was an issue if a test was announced for the end of the week. I never (when I now look back) got into another fight, as near as I can remember. Fine tuned mills (motors) were still appreciated, girls were still a huge mystery, but football wasn't.

✳ The All Important Football

Two things had my attention in high school and studies were neither of them, but at least now I tried. Football season took first place in my life for a few months of fall. We were in a five high school league and Canoga Park was the smallest. Then a buddy's father was found dead from a heartattack and his mother had in the past been killed in a car accident. My folks took Darrel in as he had nowhere else to go. He slept in the upper bunk in my room behind the garage. Darrel played football for the largest school in the league, Van Nuys. Playing them was the rival game of the year. Now I was sleeping with the "enemy."

We made a pact to never open each other's playbook

and never talk football. We ate together as a family, but he had inherited his dad's almost new car so he was gone a lot. We ate breakfast at the same table, even on game day, only with less volume. Both of us were moving closer to our game face. I really thought winning was important, as I am sure he did. It was eleven against eleven on the field and I gave it my best, and I am sure he did also. We were friends except on the field.

Fast forward to when I was a pastor serving a rather large congregation. I was standing in the lunch line at noon break on church conference business. Making idle conversation with a rather short older senior man, I was shocked to find that he had been my high school football coach. No, he had not been a deity for me, but close. I sure didn't recognize him and no evidence of recognition crossed his face as we talked. In our parting, he said he would look me up in his playbook and I tried to recall how he looked as my coach. So much for what's truly important in the teen years.

Not sure if it is Groundhog Day or The Super Bowl that has your attention. It was while we were in India I learned just how important both were in world news. I searched out five India-English newspapers and there was not a word about who had won the Super Bowl that year.

Three weeks later we returned to the US. I asked the first male I met which team had won. Have you ever had a look that said it all, "Are you an Idiot?" Yes, I have an interest in the game of football, having donned a smelly sweat-filled football uniform both in high school and a very short time in college.

In college, I found that several of the University players had just gotten out of the Service and had played football while in the Service. In fact, they made up most of the Taylor College team since all were on the GI Bill. They were big, fast, slippery, and good. Besides, I did not wish to have any one of them to have to be a bench warmer because of my taking their place. If you believe this, call me. I have a bridge to sell. (Smile here.)

It may be of interest how the game has changed. The rules in high school were where the ball came to rest, was next played from that spot. This was even if it was inches from the sideline. All the players played both offense and defense or until they were replaced or were carried off the field.

I tried out for the glory position, fullback, but was second string. I very soon found it was a position meaning the tackling dummy for the first team. My first year playing I found a difference between California and Indiana football, which was a brutal awakening. Back East the ground was stone cold, hard frozen, which was duly noted the first time I was tackled. The field was like concrete and didn't get any softer by the end of the season.

I played right guard and center. Moments I seldom or never mentioned were my high school, centering the ball over the kicker's head, or getting penalized for unnecessary roughness in the North Hollywood game, or falling for the mousetrap play against San Fernando. It was all a very long time ago when both legs and head did what they are supposed to do.

If you have read this, it is an old man recalling a time long ago when I thought football was important, and winning was all important. Maturity does modify beliefs.

❊ Bible Bravery

In review, I have left one moment out of my high school team happenings not on the field. We were in the showers at Canoga Park High School after football practice. A couple of the guys were snapping wet towels at any bare bottom handy and undefended. Our quarterback, Bob, was, and still is, a Christian. He picked up his Bible to defend himself against the sting and the red blister given by the snap of the wet towels. Fritz, a left guard (now passed away), using a vulgar language skill, called attention to what was going on. He had the whole team's attention as he berated Bob for his having and carrying a Bible.

When Bob responded, he quietly said, "Fritz, if you think it is so easy, here, you carry it." and then tossed it to Fritz. Fritz caught it and then dropped it like it would bite him.

My moment came later when I was in a crowded construction camp mess hall. I bowed my head to silently give thanks. A fellow worker, built like a brick outhouse, said something I have forgotten, but it was evident he soon expressed his disapproval of what I was doing with his fists.

We were quickly on the floor going at it hard and fast. This drew a crowd of fellow workers who no doubt figured this fight as entertainment. I remember we rolled out the mess hall door and down the steps where the fight deteriorated into just wrestling. Someone must have pulled us apart as I only remember holding my own. No memory of the aftermath, but I know I was watched by the other working stiffs at the next meal to see if I bowed my head and gave thanks. I have done this all my Christian life. My meal grace objector soon worked another shift or just avoided me, but he never bothered me again.

It was sometime later that I read I should have turned the other cheek.

※ The Three Cars

Being a teenager and having three cars was as good as it could get, or so I thought. There was a good reason for this. Old cars were cheap, so I had a car I paid ten dollars for, rescued from sitting on blocks in a chicken yard. This gave it a very unique look. and smell. It became my battered up, work car, carrying my mechanics tools, and served me faithfully. I used it to go to construction jobs and who cared how it looked? Besides, if I washed it, the shock might be too much for it, but it carried the necessary weight and didn't complain about my greasy overalls. We got along fine. It was a 1932 Chrysler Silverdome Coupe that I wish I had today because, restored, it is worth a mint.

One time I got a call from the Union to drop everything and get to the job ASAP. The problem was I had the body off of my work car. I quickly set the body on the frame and I was on my way. No problem.

Down the center of Van Nuys Blvd. was an elevated hump topped by streetcar tracks. Being in a hurry, I did not slow down going over these elevated tracks. The body of my work car, unattached, lifted up off the frame a good bit as I crossed over. A motorcycle policeman saw this and thus ended my rush to the job. The officer, after pondering how to charge me, could not find a law that said this was a no-no, so he let me go with a warning ticket. The ticket I felt was overstated as he had written, "the car body was a good foot in the air." My guess was that maybe it was less than six inches.

I got to the job, misjudged where a high-pressure gas line was, and let the ditcher operator dig into it. No explosion or ball of flame but a massive dust cloud, We both ran and I was fired. Some days are like that.

My second car was for dating. Clean and respectable,

at least in my value system. This one had a gas turn-off valve which I could operate with my foot and thus run out of gas, which mostly happened in a chosen spot. One smart young lady date just reached down and turned the valve back on. Busted. She never said yes to another date.

The third car was for competition, since my goal was to have the fastest car in the San Fernando Valley. I did everything I knew how to add horsepower, even buying special racing pistons to fit its 4-inch bore. I also added multiple carburetors, Mallery ignition, lightweight flywheel, and a host of other things. Now a reality check. A common Toyota R54 motor today has more horsepower with overhead cams and four valves per cylinder, which comes close to what was winning at The Five Hundred at the time.

In the eliminations of our top speed contention, I was paired up against a chromed everything V8, with many cubic dollars invested. He left the line a bit early and he had me by about 15 feet at the finish. I asked for a rerun because he jumped a bit on the start. For the rerun, I cut my fan belt, adding about fifteen horsepower, and he was looking at my tail lights at the finish line. Of course, I melted down the engine and had to be towed home by my friend Delbert.

❋ The Absent Windshield

Looking back to my teen years, I have no excuse except that I had a teenage brain, meaning a lack of common sense. Sure I had an excuse. My Mom was in bed with TB 24/7, dad was working in Indio, California and came home only on weekends. My younger sister was head cook, and we ate a lot of breakfast cereal.

This bit of my life was convoluted. It started with my best friend Bill spreading his fingers so the little finger and thumb drew two lines in the dust on the cab of my Model A Ford. Then he commented how much better it would look if we removed that much metal. Next came the hacksaw, welding, and making the space of four inches for the windshield. With no money to buy safety glass for any of the new windows, I sallied forth sans any glass.

Stopping at a red light, I realized there was a police car at the same light across the intersection from us. I had my roommate in the right seat. It was night, but I was very aware of not having a windshield. Picking up a rag, I began wiping my non-windshield. My friend, Darrel, also taking the hint, took a rag and reaching through the imaginary windshield, he began wiping the other imaginary side. He was either not overly bright or a joker, which he was, and a pain.

The policeman did not turn on any red lights, just made a hand motion for me to pull into a service station, where I got a world-class violation equipment ticket, no fenders, illegal headlights, no windshield, not enough road clearance, etc., and then when I started the car up to leave it was obvious I had no muffler. I was motioned back to add that to the ticket.

When dad come home who, bless him, didn't say a word when I showed him the ticket, but he did shake his head a lot. I did not get jail time but the Judge did mumble I deserved such for driving a road menace. That same friend, Darrel, later chose to become a policeman.

❀ More on the Car

This modified Ford, now with a windshield, had a rumble seat. Double dating with another good friend, Delbert, he got to sit with his date, but they did so huddled in the rumble (mother-in-law) seat.

Problem was that Dell did not have any wheels and, wanting to impress a girl, he took to criticizing my driving skills. There was no glass in the rear window so all that was said was clearly heard, especially by my date. I could not defend myself as I was facing forward and driving.

So before the next double date, I took off the housing of the steering rod. Then I removed the nut that held the steering wheel on the steering rod. Putting a power lock wrench on the steering rod right next to the floorboard, I was set.

As expected, Dell did the critical comment thing again on our next date. I undid the nut and lifted the steering wheel off of the rod, and through the glassless back window, handed the steering wheel to Dell and began steering with my feet. This was harder than I thought it would be, but with just a bit of road wobbling, I managed to stay on the road. What I was not prepared for was Dell's date's scream. It was so intense it hurt my ears. Truth is, I did not know a person could make that much noise.

No, Dell never got another date with that young lady, nor did I with my date. I do not recall her name now anyway. Delbert never mentioned any part of my driving after this event, even when there was a cause.

※ **Help! We're Drowning**

WWII was coming to an end which was the best news possible. Senior ditch day from high school was when our whole class went to a tightly held secret place. It was an awesome spot. Being sixteen had its advantages and being introduced to this rather incredible stretch of sand unknown to me, called Zuma Beach. This beach was inside information worth remembering.

Rather pleased to know about this obscure spot, I told two friends about the discovery. Each of us grabbed our sleeping bags and a few cooking tools, some firewood, and I led them to this newfound hide-a-way. It was devoid of any other ocean dippers, and this was a plus, as we planned a sleepover on the beach. We built a fire, prepared our hotdog dinner, and opened a can of something. Life was good.

The beautiful sunset quickly turned to dark. It was a moonless night with some wisps of fog and lots of salt air, seasoned with the sound of the surf. We had all expressed our manhood in the waves and after dinner were just lying around; it was as good as it could get in the teenage world.

Later that evening Darrell said, "Let's take a swim." My other friend, Jim, opted out. I sure wanted to take another dip in the ocean so I joined Darrell. We built up the fire and dove into the surf. He was a strong swimmer and eighteen, and I just barely kept up with him.

My guess is that we were at least a half-mile out or more and the Pacific swells were running about 3 feet or so. I would get my orientation as to which way it was back to the beach, via the fire. Currents would twist us around and the world for us was black, but the water was brisk and felt good and the fire was our beacon back to our camp under the stars.

Back on the beach, Jim thought it would be funny if he put out the fire -- and he did. I quickly realized I did not have the foggiest idea (no pun intended) which way it was back to the beach. I knew it was no time to panic but I sure tried to stay on top of the swells as long as I could, rubbernecking around. I called out to Darrell, and we joined up. Both of us were treading water back to back, trying to pick up any clue which way to swim back toward the beach.

Darrell, while on top of a swell, caught the pinprick of light from a car driving past on this obscure road. The two-lane road was on the other side of a growth of eucalyptus trees. This caused us to see the flickering car lights for a moment, then they were gone. I found I had been looking out to sea searching for anything that was a clue as to which way the beach might be. I had been looking toward China.

We both swam toward where the light had been seen, we thought. I had pushed myself to almost stand up to see further and was getting tired and very scared. This time it was me who saw the headlights of a fast-moving car. Then the dark returned. Swimming as hard and fast as I have ever parted the waves, we both found the beach and then catching our breath, we laid flat on the beach panting. When we got up, we let Jim live, but it was close.

I will let you guess how many times since I have given thanks to our Creator for those two cars and an ocean swell that lifted us up, when one of us for a moment was looking in the right direction. It was hard, but I forgave Jim, but never again invited him to go to the beach.

❅ Tobogganing on Thin Air

It was a joyous time because it was the end of war and back to peace. The whole youth group from CE (Christian Endeavor) now had the non-rationed gasoline to go to Big Bear Mountains for a playday in the snow. Most of the lake was frozen over and so we ice skated with all of the antics teens can think to do. We were rank amateurs but had gone to an ice skating rink several times, so we were ready for the olympics.

The most popular girl was named Ruth, (not my wife), and she *could* skate! She asked me to skate with her. She was smooth and as hard as I tried, I wasn't. My excuse was that I had on hockey skates, but that was only an excuse. She did all of the whirlings and I tried to stay up. My awareness was that the ice began to feel rubber-like, so I grabbed her and headed to shore like the speed skater I wanted to be. One of our group did punch through the ice, but it was shallow where they fell through. Ruth and I were dry, which earned us social points.

My good buddy, Bill, seeing all this, suggested something I had many second thoughts about. He had bought at a War Surplus store several internal ribs from the fuel tanks of a B 29, or so read the sign. Out of this, he made a toboggan from the beautifully curved ends on these pieces of wood.

Bill grabbed this toboggan and said, follow me. He led me to the top of a frozen waterfall he envisioned as a ski jump. Having not thought through what this really meant, nor wanting to refuse a dare, or something like that, I saddled up behind Bill.

I think it was about one third of the way down this suicide mission that the air caught the toboggan and flipped it out from under both of us. This left us midair with our legs straight out in front of us, right out of a Saturday morning cartoon show. The ever-ready law of gravity kicked in and it wasn't pretty. Neither of us broke any bones but we should have. It was a great flight while it lasted but we never tried that again, and would advise anyone else to not tempt fate this way, ever.

Thus ended a getaway day for both of us, and for a few moments of it, I thought this had to have a bad ending, and it did. Years later I gave the toboggan to a great neighbor with the promise to tell this story, adding the comment that it had strange flight character traits. I never did tell them this bit of its history. They will have to buy the book.

❋ USC vs. Notre Dame

Having been blessed with a great dad was something I never doubted. He had a rough, tough life, dropping out of grammar school in the sixth grade and going to work for the rest of his life. He passed away from a fall at eighty-two, installing a garage door opener and falling off the ladder.

He never had time to go to any sporting event, including to see me play football in high school or later in Indiana. During the war effort, he was doing what had to be done for the war work on the home front. He had a skill with a crane that few had; in the oil refineries that meant lots of overtime. I was proud of my blue-collar hard working dad.

It was after the war that I came up with a plan to have Pop see his first-ever football game. This had to be big-time, and not a game at my old high school. It had to be the top University ball at its first-string best. Because four Methodist Pastors originally formed the University of Southern California, I chose USC without question, and then their arch-rivals since 1926, "The Fighting Irish" of Notre Dame.

This was our nation's oldest football rivalry contest. The game is always scheduled to be played on the first Saturday after Thanksgiving. That year it was to be contested on the field of the Memorial L.A. Stadium Coliseum. This gave USC a home-field advantage which is a minor factor, but a bit of an edge to this grudge game.

Gameday came, and we found our seats. I invested somewhat in our fifty-yard seats; then came the waiting for the kickoff. The game was one for the books, in terms of disappointment. The final score was fifty-one for the University of Notre Dame. The University of Southern California score was zero. I never got my dad to go to any sporting event after that one. For those who may doubt this bit of my life, it was the 1966 game. Look it up.

✳ Blue Stakes

Let me begin with what I have observed. Every area of effort or specialty develops its own unique language. Each path of specialty has words that are specific to that culture, be it medicine, engineering or theology, etc. . .

At age 15 I was working in San Bernardino on the Lytle flood control as a laborer, which means pick and shovel. In a letter I wrote to my mom, I described this work. I noted that my job was "pulling witnesses while robbing the bank." I left out "while blue topping." To translate, I worked with a motor patrol (correct name for a road grader) which took dirt from the bank, in order to level the ground to meet the correct height requirements desired by the engineering plans.

These surveyor stakes had blue chalk on the top, and the grade was to be level with the top of the stake. The "witness" was the stake set apart from the grade stakes and had to be taken out so the grader could level the dirt to blue top grade. Then I replaced the "witness stake" which was to show where the grade stake might be if covered up.

Thus "I pulled the witness" stakes and then replaced them. The motor patrol operator was "Wild Bill Murphy" and without any doubt on my part, he had earned his name. He could "blue top" at 6 to 7 mph, which is a rare art and bonafide skill. You can see all of this in progress on any building site or road being built today, if you can read the stakes.

❋ The Grease Barrels

One day I came within microseconds of losing both hands. It was an intensive bit of work that had to be done early each working day. In order to keep the dirt moving equipment up and running, I had to both fuel and lubricate them and a string of cats and carryalls. This meant loading barrels of grease into the back of my assigned pickup. Never have I forgotten that each barrel of grease weighed 450 lbs. I could not load it by myself, no matter how buff I thought I was. It took two of us to do this and demanded our best effort.

A man on the dock would tip a barrel over on its side, and then roll it to a couple of 2" by 12" timbers that were set at about a 45 degree slope. The barrel was then rolled down into the back of the pickup. Another laborer and I, would stand in the bed of the pickup and stop the rolling barrel, then stand the barrel up. Next, when this was all done, I would put the grease pump into the barrel, and get to work.

This grease pump was a high powered instrument that when it was triggered, I imagined I was the tail gunner in a B17. I would shoot rapid wads of grease at any rabbit I sighted as we went to a row of waiting D8 tractors. The pump would make the appropriate machine gun sounds, and so the dawn patrol was on.

I remember a jack rabbit that didn't move. It just parted its ears, as my well aimed greasy shots kept missing. I really believe it had contempt for my effort. I could never paint a jackrabbit on the side of the pickup as a target hit.

Now, back to my story.

A barrel of grease on its side had just rolled down to us. Both of us had our hands and eyes on it, guiding and carefully controlling it after it came down the boards from the dock.

Catching a barrel, my friend let out a scream and at the same time pushed me almost out of the truck bed. In that micro moment an unseen, unsuspected barrel smashed into the first barrel. If either of us had our hands between those two barrels as they crashed rolling into each other, they would have severed or smashed our hands for sure. Strange, but my momentary thought was, "there go my violin lessons." Sorry, not true.

I have since sort of cringed when someone says something like,"offhandedly."

My fellow worker, knowing this had been done to us deliberately by the man on the dock, quietly said, "He is a mean one." Then I think he said something like, "I will take care of him." I am not sure. I never saw either of them again.

The pickup I was using was newer and it could spin donuts unlike anything I ever owned. Jumping it off of hill tops was to see how far the pickup would fly. I treated it badly, without mercy, which I have not done to anything with wheels since. I turned in the keys with a straight face.

When the job was finished, the contractors offered any pickup to my dad he might want as a reward for the great job Pop had done. He picked the one that I had beaten into the ground. Believe me I did my best in all ways possible, except honesty, to suggest for Pop to choose any other pickup, but please, please not that one.

I never did own up to this and yes, the guilt raises its ugly head now and then. But then I look at my hands and am grateful for the man who let me live my life with both of them. As a pastor I believe I would have trouble turning the page of the Bible or hymnal if this had happened. Somehow I feel that God had a bigger plan for my days on earth.

Tourists tossed coins I dove for,
and came up with a smile

CATALINA EXPERIENCE

How could a job be any better? On Catalina Island, getting off work at seven in the morning, having a free breakfast featuring three kinds of meat, then going and lying on the beach in the sun and sleeping was a teenager's delight. When the tourists arrived at the island on the Great White Steamer, I got up and swam out to dive for the coins tourists tossed. The down side of the job was not so bad, but it was pay-attention work, knowing that the man I was replacing was killed by a boulder rolling over.

The accidental death that I replaced on the job

We were loading rock onto barges for the building of the Long Beach Breakwater. If it was just one bolder, it was thirty tons or better. I called myself a "Technical Lubrication Engineer" but I was hired as an oiler. (Read, a few steps up from paid slavery.)

I was a nursemaid to a North West 80D "steam" shovel with a union card from the much coveted International Union Of Operating Engineers. Not bad for a 16 year old. I put a piece of paper in my shoe with 18 written on it so I could say I was over 18 and not lying (this is how 12 year old's enlisted in the army during the Civil War), but I did have a Dad who opened the door for me with the Union at fifteen years of age.

The best time was the sack lunch at 4:30 AM. I would go sit on the rocks and watch the waves crash and the seals play as the sun came up. I had the world on a downhill pull.

A hard-nosed Norwegian working stiff slept in the bunk above me. Old Pete took a liking to me and offered to teach me a skill I had known and in heavy construction was respected. He was a "Powder Monkey" and an artist at what he did. He could lift a massive rock by explosives and set it down where someone wanted it, or turn it into gravel. I was very interested. It was during the lesson plan on attaching a cap to a fuse line that he put the cap between his teeth and bit down, crimping the cap to the fuse, knowing there were wooden pliers to do that, which for good safety, were supplied to be used for this attachment.

I called him on this procedure and he told me in no uncertain terms that it was better to blow off your head than your hands. I backed out of becoming a powder monkey as a vocational choice. I had my second thoughts anyway, being told of two such, who still had their heads, who had loaded a house sized rock for reduction, but had not noted a soft line in the rock. As they were walking away from the blast, it went off. A slice of this rock flew and they were cut off at their knees. Rejecting this free education to handle dynamite was not a hard decision. I knew enough to know it was not for me.

July 4th was coming up and I was recalling how much fun I had with my chemistry set, making gunpowder, and putting cans over the telephone wires. It was mostly about making lots of noise on the 4th of July, and now no one would know or care if I liberated some proven big noise makers for the enviable fun of making the biggest bang on the 4th.

I knew all I needed to know about commonly used dynamite in the rock quarry, which happened often by shaking the world and breaking up the mountain into usable pieces. I had been taught by a pro the do's and don'ts of its use. I "borrowed" a number of sticks and put them in my going-home handbag with my dirty clothes. I took the water-taxi to Long Beach, then hitched a ride home. I was excited and raring to have the biggest bang of the 4th I had ever made, among the lesser firecrackers popping off.

My best friend was as excited as I was to make this a unique day to remember by what I showed him I had. But where? We decided it was the beach to do this show off. We knew it would be noticed, talked about and remembered.

At the beach we found a massive crowd and kids beyond number. We both realized it might not be the best idea to set off a really big blast in the midst of the crowd with unpredictable kids running amuck. We agreed and so drove north and found a deserted bit of ocean front, and no people. It was with somewhat of a cliff going down to a thin strip of sand and water. Perfect. At the beach cliff face we dug a small hole, and packed it with the big bang makers, all of them, then hand packed the dirt.

Having looked, and called out and still seeing no one, we lit the fuse and backed off. The result was way more than we planned or had imagined. As the dust cloud settled and some of the real-estate returned to earth, it was evident we had altered the coastline of Southern California. In a moment I knew that 60% nitro dynamite is for use on solid granite rock, not sand based soil.

The frightening surprise came as we both surveyed with some pride what we had done. Then a dirt covered figure crawled over the edge, spouting language I cannot report here. He and some girl with whom he had been practicing marriage, had been out of sight and quiet, by their choice. The "blast" rightfully had left him shaken, livid, enraged, but soon found screaming to be adequate.

No doubt a car passing by had taken this all in, then had notified some authority and they came with red lights flashing. We were either stunned or in some kind of shock, but still it was best to own up to nothing. If one or both of this couple had been killed, or even injured, we would have had this celebration in the state free housing with gray steel bars and locks as decoration. I still feel that God shakes His head and looks after teenage fools.

Later the Bible verse, Romans 8:28, leaped out at me. "And we know that all things work together for good to them that love God, to them that are the called according to his purpose." (NEB) This I knew to be true as I looked back and remembered this event.

※ Swinging Steel

My dad's occupation's pay was good. I had followed in my dad's work and there is a lot of ego satisfaction in all that is done well in heavy construction. I was 17 when a steel company hired me to be the swamper on a Lorraine Truck Crane. I was asked if I had any experience with a truck crane. I had no experience but assured them "I was born in the cab," then guessed where I should put my lunch pail that any old hand would know.

Our first job was putting up the steel skeleton framework for a high rise. The steel hangers did a job that was way beyond my fear level. A steel beam was lifted by cable to a horizontal level. The steelworkers would use a spud wrench to secure one end to keep it from tilting or swinging. Then they would walk the loose, rocking beam to the other end to do the same and this was done umpteen stories high. This could cause most men to stutter while sweating.

Before we would begin in the morning the foreman would come by and we would chat. I thought I had a new friend, or at least an important acquaintance. This went on for a week or so, then the visits stopped dead. I was told when I asked one of the guys about this sudden change, "He was just checking to see if you were sober." He had stopped checking on me when he found I did not drink, but he did now give me orders like a Master Sergeant.

There was one job that I recall with guilt. We were building a bridge and the truck crane didn't turn a wheel for two days. I was bored. Asking the boss what I could do was a mistake. He handed me a three-foot wrench and said tighten those nuts, as he pointed down. Sure enough over the edge, I could see the concrete pillars on which the bridge sat. There were six long threaded studs on each post. I was pretty sure that the nuts lying next to the studs were going to fit the wrench in my hand.

All of this would be just work. I stood on a platform hung with four long cables. The problem was as I either pushed or pulled, the platform moved in the other direction. Then there was the openness under the slanting or swinging six-ply I was standing on. Tightening the nuts was somewhat exciting. Now the guilt. Not all, if any, of those nuts were run down by me to specs or code.

I had to face the boss and he asked the obvious. I lied. Every time I drive across that bit of highway, I remember my lie and wonder if the nuts were ever cinched down.

❋ Under the Sky

Working south of Gorman, on the Ridge Route, I was camped out in a valley by a small stream. I had my rifle, tent, sleeping bag, and was eating at the Big Lemon Cafe. It couldn't get any better. I was making big money for a seventeen-year-old and loving it all. The scale was one dollar and twenty-five cents an hour and lots of overtime. The benefits were the stars at night where I made camp. Having lived in the wonderful land of the desert where you could almost reach up and get a handful of stars most any night, it was almost that good here.

I would meet the maintenance crew, the dirty dozen, at the Big Lemon for breakfast. There were six of us and it was heavy, dirty work, so we did the work of twelve. Coffee was five cents for a bottomless cup. It was noticed that I was putting cream in my coffee, to which the foreman commented, "Well, that divides the men from the boys." I never put cream in my coffee again until college, remembering that once I had liked it and still do.

I was soon sleeping outside of my tent just under the cosmic wonder of a clear night sky. I picked up a Newspaper at breakfast and did a double-take that changed it all: "Hunter Shot." The shooter thought the victim in a sleeping bag was a deer. It was hunting season, but the poor guy sleeping in his bedroll was dead. I skipped the night sky in my pup tent from that time on. I am a slow learner but the lesson does not have to be given twice.

✳ The Turnaround

I was sitting on the seat of a backhoe at the end of a job, having brought the hoe back to the storage yard. I was faced with the big decision. I was being paid universal equipment operator's wages, the maximum on the pay scale. I knew then that I could quit and go back to school or I could make a pile of money, buy or build more cars, each of which had its attractions. Going on to college was foolish, because even thinking about the ministry was laughable for a very simple reason. I knew I could never speak in public. But I knew I could be a building missionary.

When I asked Dad about going to college, he was quiet for a long time, and finally he said something like, "If you must." We both knew it was the end of G.L.Truman and Son Construction Company, because the son had signed out.

III

COLLEGE AND SIMPSON BIBLE INSTITUTE

❋ Me? Bible School?

I finished my first year in engineering and I liked all of it, the physics, chemistry, math, but not English. My friend Bill Cooper had gone to school under the Christian and Missionary Alliance (C&MA), in Seattle, Washington, where people were trained for overseas missionary service. Bill wrote me a glowing, enthusiastic letter about how great it was. It was described as wonderful in all parts, and caused me to temporarily change my education direction. Bill was aware that I knew next to nothing about the Bible. So according to Bill, I needed to opt out of engineering to enroll in three years of Bible study as a life time investment, then finish engineering. This was life changing.

The only time I rode the Greyhound bus was to get to Seattle and on to where Simpson Bible Institute was located (now named Simpson University and is in Redding, California). My mother had purchased a large trunk and filled it with all sorts of things that we thought I would need and we decided it would be difficult to hitchhike with a trunk, so it was Greyhounding for me.

Simpson then was a small school compared to Los Angeles City College and I liked it. There I had been assigned seat #254 in a chemistry lecture. Uproarious applause broke out one time during a lecture when it was announced with great excitement that the Periodic Table was closed. Big schools sometimes get it wrong.

At Simpson, each of us was assigned a job. As an out of state person and engineering as my goal, my assigned job was collecting the garbage. Thus the nickname hung on me was "Hector the garbage collector." I still have that moniker in e-mails from fellow classmates. The other job I was tagged with was pots and pans washup after the evening meal. Second-year I was assigned the night watchman and missed a lot of sleep.

The third year they made me Assistant Dean of Men. Perhaps they wanted to keep track of me? On weekends I worked moving sawdust to holding bins for cheap heat, or anything where I could earn a dollar. My dad could see some value in engineering but not any value to Bible school, so this was all on my own. My backup job was roofing and in the winter this got to be dicey. One job was on a steep church roof. It was colder than I thought possible with intermittent rain, then snow which made the roof beyond slippery. They did not have to gift wrap my paycheck on this job as I knew I had earned every cent twice over, and never again.

One joy was knowing and spending time with the Dean of Women, Mrs Koenigswald. She was a missionary widow. While in Tibet her husband was driving a jeep and a sniper bullet hit the spoke of the steering wheel, then slid off, killing him. She was indeed a saint with a twinkle in her eye and she enjoyed life. I loved her for the joyful person she was in my life when I was assistant Dean of Men.

A joyful group of friends who
enjoyed singing in concert

✳ Head First

This confession business is soul cleansing and a bit painful. Maybe that is why in every church service I put together, I had a written general confession and time for soul searching for private prayers. Besides, the Methodist Order of Service calls for a prayer of confession.

Jack stood next to me in our college choir, and he was tall, dark, and handsome. He had the body of a gymnast and the voice of a classic baritone. The problem was Jack (not his name) didn't want to be a student at this highly disciplined religious college. His parents wanted him to be in this student body because he needed the discipline. He rebelled as much as he could, mostly in very creative ways, which I came to quietly admire.

I liked Jack and we became bonded buddy friends, but there was tension because I was the assistant Dean of

Men. I had to try to stay one step ahead of him and do it without knowing too much, lest I learned something that would come to the Dean's attention. Jack had a dorm room to himself, and after-hours would slip out of the dorm, go off-campus to who knows where, and return at all hours. I had a real hunch about what was happening.

1. I had to get his attention.
2. I had to confront him because he was on the edge of being expelled.
3. I had to think about it and come up with a plan.

I sure wasn't going to wait up for him as he slipped back into the dorm and vaulted his body into his top bunk. So I took out all the bolts of his war surplus wooden bunk bed. I thought the noise of the boards coming loose would wake me. He had a thick rug so no one else would wake up because of any noise. Jack had the habit of flipping himself into the upper bunk with a jump and a half roll. The head of his bed was toward the window, which I opened to let him know that something was afoot. I then hit my bed and I was gone.

I heard the crash and then a scream that could peel paint. I hit the floor running, and threw open Jack's door to discover that the window end of the bed had collapsed, making a perfect chute, sending Jack head first out a second-story window. Thinking fast, he had spread his legs as he left his dorm room via the open window. I found him upside down, hanging by his spread legs. It was a shock seeing just his bare feet greeting me, and Jack helpless, screaming bloody murder with words never heard on that campus.

I started to laugh instead of going to his rescue. To add insult, he only had his briefs on. The third and fourth floors were the girl's domain. A number of ladies opened their windows and heads appeared, wanting to know what all the blood-curdling screaming was about.

About then I realized this was truly a life or death situation if he dropped headfirst to the ground, and that was when I stopped laughing and pulled Jack back into his dorm room. My real issue? Was Jack going to kill me?

I left the next day with the choir for the Spring Tour and never again saw my friend I almost killed, because he was expelled. Recalling this I find myself smiling because then it was and still is… a funny story that came too close to tragedy.

✳ My Twenty-First Birthday

While on spring choir tour, I was approaching twenty-one years old, and Mom fixed and sent a lavish Mother box of home baked goods for my birthday (BD). Ever since my youngest days my mother had made me what as a child I called "Rubber Cake," which is known as Angel Food Cake, for my natal day. When Mom made it she would add a boiled dime to the mix, which I never got, but those who did at my birthday parties were excited. Mom had included such a cake in my BD box.

When I got back from the choir tour, the box was in my dorm room, but it only held crumbs. My good friends said they had a grand birthday party for me in my absence. I quietly hoped whoever got the dime chipped a tooth.

All of this happened before my BD date rolled around. At the Dean's staff meeting held in the Women's Dean's office and meeting on my big day, I tried to be quiet about my birthday. The Women's Dean was to me our in-resident angel. Mrs Koeningswald had gray hair, the spirit of an eighteen year old and the wisdom of an ancient. But best of all, she topped it off with a wonderful sense of humor. I liked her more than anything.

After business, and the Dean noting it was my 21st, everyone sang the traditional and she presented me with an "Angel Food" cake with 21 candles. I was a man by the years but the clock turned back a lot of years as I was serenaded. All this hit me right in the center of my emotions. They said this cake was all mine, so I was to take it to my room and share it with whomever I chose. Covering my BD gift as much as I could, I made it to my room, and locked the door. The candles had been lit and blown out, and wishes made. Now it was just me, lots of memories and gratitude, looking at this special unexpected gift.

I had a knife and started to cut my special cake. It didn't happen, because it was an Angel Food pan covered with soap suds. I now, not then, remember with a smile the humor that came with my entering my adult years, and now am grateful for the smile, even laughter it brings as I sawed away on that pan, wanting a piece of BD cake.

Come on, this is good humor that has lasted into my old age. Even now as I write, sharing this, I am smiling.

※ **Favorite Sport**

It started by going through some old family pictures when I saw something never spoken of by my dad. It was of him as a skier coming off of a ski jump in Steamboat Springs, Colorado. He was in mid air making a distance record jump. This picture now hangs in the museum in Steamboat Springs. Two days before he died, he said this record jump was because he fell further than anyone else.

Being desert raised I had never heard of skiing but the seed had been well planted. It sprouted in the winter of my first year study at Simpson. It blossomed when it snowed for three days straight. In town I saw a pair of antique skis in a war surplus store. They had wooden edges and bear trap bindings, at a give-away price. I soon found that bargains can be very expensive in many ways. This lesson came as the bus driver leading back to the school would not let me on the bus with my skis. It meant an eight mile hike and I started back to school on foot.

It was then that my English teacher, driving back to school, recognized me trudging along and stopped for me and the skis. My world went from blisters to smiles. Having learned our common language with double negatives etc, being normal, I was one of her major teaching challenges.

Yes, I had taken "Dumb-Bell English" in my first year in college along with calculus, chemistry, physics and engineering, but the English class didn't take. During the welcome ride with my English teacher, and small talk, I asked her a serious question. "What do you suggest I do with my life?" Her answer is still very clear in my memory book. She took her eyes off of the road for a moment, looked at me and said "Be a jackhammer operator."

What she did not know was that I had done that, with iron towed boots and all. I never saw that as a lifetime choice. Her words really rocked my world. It was twenty years or so later that at a reunion banquet we happened to be seated together at the head table, and she remembered me. I casually brought up that I was nationally syndicated with Copley News Service. It was a sweet moment. I was very careful to not inform her that I saw to it that I had married a wife who could spell, and always hired a secretary who was very good in English to do the finish copy of all articles submitted.

The skis did look good hanging on my dorm wall but they were bought to use, so I bought a second pair. Then I noised it about so those who were going skiing could invite me and my second pair of skis, which they could use. It worked! Soon we were on our way to Snoqualmie Pass for my first time ever to ski, and my visions of swishing the mountain slopes was real.

I soon mastered the bunny slope with a rope tow pulling me up a very small hill. I had the barstool turn down pat (swing my body to make the turns). This works great up to fifteen miles an hour. Faster than this speed on the slope, it absolutely guarantees that it ends in a crash, a head plant or most often, a hospital.

Ego called at that moment because I was with classmates. I then moved over to the advanced ski lift with confidence. Up and up and up into the forest and clouds to a destination of getting off safely among the trees. There was a narrow ski path winding down. It was my bunny slope mastery (ski walking) that led me on. The trail opened up to a steep place which presented a major drop in elevation. This led to the unwelcomed increase in uncontrolled speed at this point (read panic), void of trees, for real hot dog skiing for those who knew how this was done. Not being in control, I went up and over a huge snowbank, and was airborne for a moment. I grabbed a tree as I went by and became a tree hugger some several feet off the ground. I slid down the tree and made it down off the mountain by walking.

Moral: Take a basic How To Ski Lesson the first time you "strap on the boards." It truly is the most exciting (and expensive sport) I have ever found.

❋ A Day Off

It was a day off. I had been roofing and the paycheck was burning a hole in my pocket. It was late in the season and before spring hit I wanted to try a ski trail I had only heard about. You had to hike to where you came across the trail going down off the mountain.

I grabbed my ski buddy, Bill. He knew what was on my mind. It was one place on a high lift that when you got off you could hike much higher. We had talked about it making a really long run, so I said let's do it.

It was a longer hike than I had figured, but it did open up the side of the mountain with a straight shot down. Being late, it was half price, and we could get in one really good long run.

We found the trail to hike higher. I rested in the shade under a big pine. Bill took a picture of me that was put in the school annual wearing my war surplus outfit. We took off basically flat out racing. Coming up over a ridge there was a girl who had fallen and was half getting up. Bill motioned me to the right of her and we both passed her flat out which had to have scared her. That was the intent.

I couldn't help it. I glanced back at our victim and hooked a ski edge, cartwheeled, crashing and bouncing down the slope. Justice was done as I had to have a body cast for several weeks.

※ The Women's Assistant Dean

One line of the fine print of my new job as Assistant Dean at Simpson, was to be at the head table in the dining room for breakfast. The same requirement was for the assistant women's dean. Why? The Deans lived off-campus and had their breakfast at their own home table. We two assistants alternated saying grace and keeping the peace.

I never knew my counterpart at any level. She was not a student and was thirty plus years and going on pushing fifty. To convey her authority, she always wore her hair in a tight bun, always dressed in black or gray, and wore a stern look that could stop a clock. Later, as a Psych major, I still hadn't figured her out, except, never smiling, she had to be one unhappy person.

The following is a regret, and the truth only told to my wife Ruth, and anybody now reading what I did years ago. It started with the keys. We both had free campus roaming privileges. Not sure what tipped me off, but it seemed she might be into the desert goodies under lock and key in the kitchen, a kingdom ruled over by the head cook who we called Sargent behind her back. Checking the inventory several times, I was sure of it. Noting what was always missing was one item: a blueberry muffin. Setting one out on a saucer I loaded it. I acquired five kidney pills that I was assured would do no harm but would turn the assistant dean's urine blue.

The next day in our Dean's meeting, I believe I drew blood biting my lip trying to keep a straight face. There were only two people who knew what I knew, and no doubt her doctor knew what was going on.

This in no way could I ever own up to after I realized all of the implications. She never seemed trim and officially proper after this event, and maybe her doctor is still shaking his head. But I always smiled at her, even when she was at the head dining room table speaking of private information under office wraps. I once passed along a saucer of milk to her while we were doing our thing, and she was passing along information, and being catty. She got the insult. I just smiled but thought of what only she, the Doc and I knew.

❈ What is that Smell?

At Simpson, two brothers roomed together and had remodeled their dorm room to be the envy of the dorm, and they knew it. Also they had spent some time in Tijuana, which is the sailor's goal, where all of the sins of the flesh are for sale. In other words, they were worldly-wise and they were sure of it.

They made a big deal of again painting their room a different shade of red with a new kind of paint that had just come on the market, Kemtone. I arranged for them to be called to the phone in the college reception room. I had gotten a pitcher of milk, so while they were answering my phony telephone call, I entered their room. They had started painting so I just mixed the milk into the paint and left.

As I figured, in time the milk would sour. Soon I could smell it out in the hall and it got worse. My little secret prank came to an end when they knocked on my door and asked if they could sleep on the floor in my room, as the smell was so bad in their room.

I mumbled something about this new paint being really terrible and said yes. I was one of several others who scrubbed their walls and finally applied a sealer.

No, I have never owned up to what happened, I just learned a lesson that what seems an innocent prank and funny may not be so for others.

❈ Horns and Halos

Let me continue this bit of my Simpson years by noting something that is an absolute fact about human nature. All of us are a mixture of horns and halos, yes, in different proportions, but this is our lot as mortals.

If you sense that I am going to own up to my horns, you are so right. This was when dirty tricks were thought funny and were popular, which is my only defense (read excuse). The receiving end was my roommate at Simpson. He was my pastor's son and we both had been into building fast, competitive cars, which we often tested.

Dave had distinguished himself by setting a rope climbing record at Van Nuys High. The last time I checked, it still stands. He was built like he should be a record holder. Bill, my ever best friend who had introduced and enticed me to take time out to study the Bible, was also my ski buddy. Dave had never been on skis. We invited him to join Bill and myself to go skiing with us, teaching him how. He went along trusting us, which was a mistake.

We took Dave to the very top of the mountain. We explained it was much like riding a bicycle. Really slow riding is hard but you go fast till you learn how, then slow ski. He looked down between his skis at this expert run, then looked at us both. We gave him a thumbs up and he pushed off over the edge. In a moment he knew he had been had. He yelled so loud that his yell may still be echoing along with some very explicit choice words I never knew he knew.

The wonder was that he made it to the lower level where there was a knee-high growth of pine trees. They whipped and slapped his legs as he plunged on. His yell at this point could drown out a jet. He lost his balance and went down in a cloud of snow in the air, for sure, head over tea cup.

What I had not figured out was I now had to sleep with one eye open. I bunked with Bill, sleeping on the floor for a week. Returning to the dorm I knew whatever the retaliation was to be, I had earned it. Dave was smart enough to know my waiting for retaliation was his payback. It worked.

To catch a few winks of a nap, slipped in before dinner, was a gift. This stolen moment of sleep was necessary. A hall loudspeaker always brought my slumber to an end. Without thinking, I rolled out of the top bunk, stiff legged, and hit the floor flat footed, or at least I thought I had hit the floor. This procedure was normal and was satisfying as the wooden floor of the old dorm always complained loudly.

What I didn't know was that Dave was giving himself an enema and I had landed flat footed on the enema bag. He insisted thereafter that he had an awful taste in his mouth. He later would catch me at some serious moment and would frown looking at me. Then Dave would run his tongue across his teeth making a face. I did not always keep from bursting out laughing, with those around us having not a clue as to what the joke was.

✳ Thanksgiving That Did Not Happen

It was the national day to stop and give thanks for our nation's blessings and to do it with family and friends while feasting. My friend Bill and I could stay on campus and eat campus food. Then we received an invitation to join a family for this day's celebration.

The exciting part was that the 'come join us' was on Vashon Island, some 12.5 miles away as the fish swam. This was no problem, we would rent a boat and row over to the happy feast, boardering on the edge of forgivable gluttony. The best thing was it would not resemble institutional food.

We rented a rowboat and left early to make it a

leisurely day of relaxation. The bay was calm, the sky was a painter's choice for a great canvas. We found a rhythm that moved us right along as we both shared what we were most thankful for, interspersed with speculation of what our families were preparing at that moment, which led to our recalling Thanksgivings past. We even rested on our oars as we had rowed down this memory path.

Then it happened. Getting moving again we both put our backs into the task. That is when Bill on the port side of our craft fell over backward with the oar still in his hand. The oar lock had ripped out and the oar was now just an awkward piece of wood moving us to our Thanksgiving dinner.

With one good oar, you row in circles. After several going nowhere efforts, we realized it was best to head back to home port, which we found was easier said than done. A breeze came up in the afternoon, ruffling the bay, and we found currents that had caused no notice when our craft was in our control. Not dressed for the cold evening chill with spitting rain, we were glad to get a tow back to port.

The campus was empty of all living souls, and the kitchen was locked up. I had a key but just wanted to get warm.

Angels must chuckle when we mortals confidently make our plans.

✳ Alone with Joy

Having never been inside of anyone's head, I can only vouch for this very isolated memory from 1949. I think it happened after making my last rounds of the campus as the night watchman, that I faced a massive snowfall which had dumped during the night. I knew it was a record and

I knew it would shut down the campus and even Seattle, for sure.

All of this was met with my response of getting my skis and the thought of not having to pay for any lift ticket, just ski. As the sun came up, nothing was moving or could. The campus was on a high ground named Phinney Ridge, overlooking most of Seattle. My twist of brain cells spoke with the words that this was a once in a lifetime opportunity, not to be passed by. That was all that it took.

There was not a car, bus or a fellow mortal footprint to be seen. It truly was a record depth of powdery virgin snow covering everything, and it was all mine. So it was tuck and go.

Addictive escape

Skiing was pure joy as I went through red traffic lights, took my half out of the middle, blew through intersections and never picked up red and blue lights behind me. In spots I was sure that I was over 25 mph with a grin of pure fun. There was a thought that it would be great to get a speeding ticket for excessive speed on a city street with no driver's license asked for: " Your Honor, I was on skis."

It all came to an end in Ballard, and I began my slowdown through a hotel parking lot and ended like a ski run throwing snow, as I turned sideways on the lake dock. This has all has been savored and a number of times remembered on crowded ski slopes and sleepless nights. The odd thing is I have never once had a moment's recall of how I got back up to Phinney Ridge. A ski run of a lifetime is never forgotten.

✳ Social Polish of a Dirt Clod

Being in college, and paying my own way, meant there was only time for study and as much work as I could find. Translated, no girlfriend. One small redhead did get my attention when I was a Simpson senior. No, we had never held hands, but I swallowed twice and asked her to go with me to hear Arturo Rubinstein, a classical pianist, in concert. I felt I had a high-level chance she could not say no, at least that was my hope. But this had two problems.

First, I had sold my three cars to help with tuition. This impediment was solved by asking my good friend, Bill, to borrow his 1934 Hudson-Terraplane which wasn't running. The price was to fix it. After hearing the sweet sound of a motor purring, I, in my greasy, snow-wet work clothes was inexcusably late, but the car ran like a champ.

She had been waiting for me in the reception area. I sure didn't look like I was ready for a concert hall or a first date. She was not only ready for the date, but had a sparkle in her eyes, and no doubt with a touch of something girls have but I could not dare get close enough to tell, called perfume. I was stammering to find words explaining my "Terrible pain" problem.

She looked me over and never said a word. Not smiling, she turned, and went up the stairs to her room. I did not attend the concert but realized at that moment that God's plan for me was that maybe I was to be a celibate construction missionary. I could see in her eyes that I had the social polish of a dirt clod.

Quickly the year came to an end as did my time of training to be a missionary. I had made a life switch from engineering and now had been accepted as a missionary candidate by the C&MA mission board. My life was on hold when I returned home while I waited for my mission assignment. I knew this was God's calling, but I was still asking for direction.

✳ Billy Graham Movie

He had bailed out of his wounded B17 and did some time as a POW. After peace came, he became the Vice President of Don-Lee Studios. I was standing next to him after church when he asked me if I wanted a job. "Sure," was my quick response and a whole new world opened up for me. I was 21 and why shouldn't I? Dick Ross hired me to do whatever.

Finding that he had left the world of TV and was putting together a film company called "Great Commission Films," made me sure I had made the right choice. This name was in response to Acts 1:8., "Go into all the world and proclaim the Good News." He was a Christian and this was his commitment. In what had been a garage he showed me how to use a Moviola. I had just graduated from Simpson as a newly minted missionary, with missions on my agenda, and I was on the cutting edge which had opened up to me in God's own way.

Robert (Bob) Pierce, founder of World Vision International, 1950, was in China as a missionary sending back film. My new job was to make a documentary film out of what was sent to my boss. This was easier said than done. One reason was that I felt Bob was using his movie camera like a garden hose. I did the best I could. At Universal Studios we only shot with the use of very heavy tripods. Most often they were anchored. My job was to move such around according to the changing whim of anyone calling themselves a director. I saw no future there.

The film I was asked to make was entitled "China Challenge." I felt it really was a learning challenge that had been made for me. Next, we made "Japan Welcomes The Word." The script called for an opening shot of the atomic explosion which I painted, but you had to use your imagination...a lot. This was for the American Bible Society.

Starting on the next film, I was told to drop everything. We were going to Portland, Oregon to do a film of Billy Graham in his second crusade, following the big one here in L. A.

I found you could rent everything to make a movie. All items that were needed were packed into a truck and trailer. I grabbed my hat and headed for Portland without a valid truck driver's license, but I did hit the road with a big soul-satisfying smile thinking this could be fun.

Two events I remember getting to Portland. On the Oakland Bay Bridge where it curves, a car came at me on my side of the bridge. Risking trailer whip I moved quickly to the other side of the bridge road and quickly back. For a moment it was headlight for headlight.

Unloading and setup was chaos. I found the Graham team was all housed on the same hotel floor. Having never seen or heard about Billy Graham, I had the image of an Elmer Gantry. I soon saw that he was absolutely a straight arrow. I was impressed with his rules. I recall one about never entering an elevator if there was a lone woman in there. I also noted the handling of money. A Portland company handled all the money in and out. He passed my test.

I got my picture in the papers. I was high in the rafters with a klieg light on my shoulder. We were ready to film.

What a Preacher!

✳ Billy Graham Rally

The preparation for the Billy Graham rally was intense. Each night the demands of the Crusade had our full attention. Graham was an incredibly gifted speaker and the people's response to his message was impressive. Great numbers of fellow mortals either were accepting Christ into their lives or wanted to rededicate their life to Christ. This meant it was often midnight before things wound down and the last life searcher to become a follower of Jesus was prayed for. Then we changed the lighting, moving the klieg lights around, setting up for a different take.

Rev. Graham wanted to do a personal shot for the film. I had been in the pulpit with him doing the clapboard and saved that film clip. I have it somewhere, maybe.

Now I sat right under the camera lens facing the Rev. I was to hold up six fingers and drop one each minute he spoke. All of this without a script at one a.m. or so in the morning. I became so engrossed in what he was saying that I forgot to drop a finger as time moved along and when we ran out of film, he said, "OK, reload and let's do it again".

I should have been fired.

Cliff Barrows, gifted member of Billy Graham team

Cliff Barrows, the song leader for the Crusade, was about my age, dynamic and dramatic. He impressed me so much when he gave a Children's Sermon in the afternoon program that I often copied his style when I had my own pastoral appointment.

My personal high point was hearing George Beverly

Shea sing a hymn at the crusade I had never heard before. It was "How Great Thou Art" and it resonated with me at soul level. The next morning I asked Shea if I could join him for breakfast and of course he said yes. We talked and ate, then I asked him if I could pay for his breakfast so I could always know that I did. He smiled and said "OK" and I'm still glad that I did.

The next Crusade was being planned for Texas. I had to make a hard decision. My problem at this point was I had been in college for four years, one in engineering, and three in the (unaccredited) study of the Bible. Obviously I had been changed and was ready for the mission field, but without a degree. I was heavily advised by the mission board that such a degree was not necessary.

Thinking otherwise, I had applied at several colleges to transfer and finish earning a degree. I met a Taylor University (TU) student who recommended Taylor - so I applied, then found out he had been asked to leave TU. I forgot about Taylor.

The big decision? To continue making films with the Graham team or go to college? Time ran out and all the schools I had been accepted to were now closed to me as their roster was filled. TU did not answer my inquiries so it seemed the logical place to go as it was the only place I had not gotten a rejection letter. Problem was that I had sold all of my cars, so that left my thumb to get to Indiana and TU.

It was the best thing ever and in two years I had a degree and my life partner. God's guidance in all of this is beyond question in my walk of faith.

IV

TAYLOR UNIVERSITY

※ Upland, Indiana

I was offered a ride in exchange for driving east as far as Taylor. I still wanted that degree, so taking my courage in both hands, I took a risk. Was this where I was supposed to go, or was it one more closed door?

With the car's owner and me driving straight through I arrived on campus in the early a.m., found an unlocked car, curled up in the back seat, and slept till the sun woke me. Dressed in my motorcycle boots, Levis, T-shirt, and no doubt smelling like a goat, I took a deep breath and found the Admissions Office.

Now the act was to have them believe they had admitted me. Yes, they did not have any of the required paperwork or an on-campus room for me, but they had an off campus house just rented and there I found friends I had never met.

Then came a job washing dishes, an interview with the coach about playing football, and the college tradition of having a blind date social with it being the girl's choice. I told the one who had picked me that I was celibate. She looked at me again, and we went on and had a good time, and I had a life direction. I was satisfied and on my way but, I did look around. There was one young lady who was gorgeous, but so what?

The next night was a review of college talent and it was a boisterous good show with lots to applaud. Then the stage darkened and a poet was introduced. This was a turnoff until this very same good looking, talented mortal was standing center stage dressed in a white flowing gown, and in the spotlight. A hush fell as she began reciting a poem I had never heard. It got my attention. As she said the words, it was with meaning, and she was looking straight at me. Looking back, that was when she either offered or set the to-be-married hook. Either way, my life and hers changed directions ever after together, because I swallowed that to-be-married hook right down to the sinker.

Ruth's response in her words:

I saw Lee bounding up the stairs to the registration hall and was immediately attracted. Never had I dated a guy who wore blue jeans and boots; this was different. He fit my model guy: tall (6'2"), great body, blue eyes, blondish hair, great smile. So when I teamed up with his roommate for the blind date social, Lee and his date kept coming over to talk to us. A couple of days later I was walking back from class with his date and she told me he was 'celibate'. As soon as I got to my room I looked up the word: a man who would not marry for religious reasons. I slammed the dictionary shut and said aloud, "There's no such man!"

When I saw him and his roommate in the second row at the talent show, I admit I spoke my best poem directly to him:

"Thou art not my first love/ I loved before we met/ The memory of that summer song is pleasant to me yet./ No, thou art my last love/ my sweetest and my best./ My heart but shed its outer leaves to give thee all the rest." (A.J.Sampson, 1831-1929)

Back to Lee:

I was on a slippery slope but I didn't care and wasn't sure what was happening. Sometime in the next week, I asked her to go for a walk, as I was basically broke, and with the apprehension of her just turning around and walking away seemed to be the expected. She accepted! We went for a walk and it started to rain. We took shelter under an old oak tree.

That is when it happened. I kissed her and she kissed me back. Beyond WOW, I had a case of the "happies" on steroids. I told my roommates I got to hold her hand, and I got the ribbing that it called for. I found all of my skivvies stapled together. I smiled and wondered what all of this meant with the most attractive female on campus.

From then on I made an excuse to be with her every chance I could.

Like being on a rogue river raft, things were happening which only felt like we were in some kind of control. First, we were both classed as juniors, so there was a two-year wait to be married. Second, she was a Methodist pastor's daughter. Being the wife of a missionary was not a problem for her, if not a plus. I wrote the C&MA Mission Board of my possible change of plans, thinking that a wife who wanted to go to the mission field was great, even if she wished to remain a Methodist, which I saw as no problem.

By return mail I received notice that I was dropped from

the accepted candidate's list. In that one letter the ground under my feet was no longer there. This earthquake to my world left me nothing to stand on. I was outside any church home and my future just evaporated. What I had planned and prepared for was no more.

❊ Home For Christmas

One of the residual marks left by WWII was the widespread use of hitchhiking. Servicemen had almost instant rides, as did I with books under my arm. When I was at my engineering class at Cal State L.A, this was my daily ride. So no problem wanting to get home from Taylor University in Indiana, as this was the way I got there, in one ride.

I took a green window shade and in bold white letters, wrote, "CALIF, HOME, XMAS." The first crisis came along about St. Louis, when I found that no personal checks can be cashed from out of town. Mom had sent me a $10 check which made going home for Christmas possible. The financial situation tightened up for me.

The second lesson was by a driver who picked me up -- and I soon fell asleep. He changed his mind, and at 2 a.m. dropped me way north of where he said he was going. I found there was snow in patches on the ground where I was dropped. I tried to stay warm and the sunrise was never so welcomed as was the first light.

Walking, I came across a church and on the other side off the road, I hoisted my thumb and was ready for a ride. I saw these church folk come to Sunday School, then those who came to church, then after service, leave. No one offered me anything. A whole lot of homesickness set in.

That evening, two dudes who had too much to drink picked me up. I was in the back seat and a loose U-joint was trying to do its best to join me in that seat. This ride was unlike any I ever had, it was just hanging on and praying. I was glad to disembark from an accident that hadn't decided where to happen.

Later that night I was again picked up by a man who drove at night with his lights off, turning them on at the last minute for oncoming traffic. He enjoyed scaring oncoming drivers, and me. I arrived in Amarillo, Texas with the thought that there had to be a better way.

I found that this was the center for used car distribution, so I signed up. You ride free, just get the car to California at your expense. First, leaving town, I was stopped by the police. He wanted to see my permit to drive a dispatched car. He named a cost now forgotten that was impossible. He said to turn back and get the expensive permit, and I did turn back, but with limited funds, left Amarillo by back roads heading west. I saw a lot of sagebrush and oil wells on rural Texas roads while evading the police.

A roadside sign said "Gas." I filled up because it was six cents a gallon. They called it Wellhead gas. I knew kerosene when I smelled it. It worked as long as you never turned the motor off or let it idle for more than five minutes. This got me through the part of Texas where it seemed hell would be a local call.

By New Mexico I was so hungry I stopped at a country store and asked/begged for something to eat. The owner gave me a raw potato, and it kept my body and spirit together. I picked up a hiker, and because I was sleepy, let him drive and when I woke up, the sun was in my eyes. I knew we were headed East, not West, and so we parted, wanting to go in different directions.

The main street of Phoenix, AZ. was lined with orange trees with big oranges on every branch. Waiting till I would not be seen, I harvested all I could hold, then found they were not edible, but were roadway decoration.

Because of this long ordeal to get home, I learned to advertise as a driver or found a program to drive a car either way across the country, only paying for gas. I always filled up with Wellhead gas and kept going. I found that new cars were more fun and on delivery such cars' odometers were turned back to almost zero. The new owners were told to keep their speed below 50 mph the first five hundred miles or so. This way to get a ride worked until they began to manufacture cars in California.

I eventually made it home for Christmas, and it was worth it. Mom's homemade pies and good conversation did lead me to mention that I had met a wonderful girl.

We announced that we planned to be one. It has lasted 69 years so far.

✳ Now the World Knows

Back at school and only six weeks after that fateful poem, I asked Ruth to marry me. And with her eyes sparkling, thank God, she said yes and did not walk away. Later she told me that she was also thinking if she was willing to wash my socks and shorts and it was that lifelong yes she committed to. On campus we were just another couple going 'steady' and only we knew better. If anybody paid attention they might have caught on.

Easter break brought a trip to Michigan to meet her parents, and be grilled by her dad, who wasn't sure he wanted to marry off his daughter to this broke stranger from California. He did this in his office in the basement for what seemed like hours. Either I passed or he gave up.

It was supposed to be a secret, but Ruth and I seemed to be chosen to announce our engagement at the Jr-Sr. banquet. Before dessert was to be served we slipped out into a dark hallway. We were to return with her wearing an engagement ring and me with a triumphal smile. it seemed to me, I also should have had my pockets turned inside out.

I had picked out the ring sometime before and had been making payments on it seemingly forever. Even so, the rock still looked so small that it was like asking her to feel the rough spot, and saying that is the diamond. In the dark, I lied and tried to be up to the moment which meant an awful lot to her. I said the ring was not ready as I slipped it onto her finger, "so here is a ring till I can get the one I bought."

In a flash Ruth took her hand back and without a mumbled word of thanks or a kiss on my cheek, spun around and ran into the girl's restroom. Her explanation later was that she was not going back into that banquet room with a dime store ring.

I figured that I had just been stomping on thin ice but it hadn't broken through; it was close. And there was our senior year yet to get through.

✳ A Trance to Remember

It was announced on the bulletin board at Taylor, and happening at the same time as my history class. A hypnotist was going to hold forth in a small group. I chose to go and check it out. I got my only D for cutting history class but was glad I did. With his instruction, I learned how to hypnotize.

The first thing learned was no one under trance would do anything against their basic values. Second, it was more dangerous than I ever knew and used it only a very few times in ministry. I had become a psychology major so this was research for me.

Here was my first shock. I hypnotized my roommate after asking him. He was a good subject and was quickly under. I told him to write his name as he did as a twelve-year-old. He did, but it was a name I had never heard him use. Suddenly I was learning something that was none of my business.

Wish I had stopped there, but it was a whole new field I had never been anywhere near. Knowing this will be hard to believe, but here it is anyway. With him in a hypnotic state, I made a minor cut on his arm, told him not to bleed, and he didn't. This had been demonstrated in the lecture and I didn't believe it was real. It was. Then using a sharp item like a darning needle, I ran it into his leg calf with the same command, and no bleeding, not a drop.

By now all of those reading this are giving thanks that their roommate wasn't me. My roomie never knew any of this. If he had, I would have had to sleep with one eye open, clutching a club.

I did one more test of what I had seen in the lecture. My roomie was slightly built. The teacher said no one could be hypnotized against their will. This was checked out for being truthful by taking him from natural sleep to a hypnotic sleep. Proof this was not true.

Then what to do? I put his head on a chair and his heels on another chair, telling the poor guy to be stiff and straight. He was like a board and I even sat on him at about his belt line. My two-hundred and six pounds didn't bend him an inch.

About this time I realized I was into an area where I was way, way over my head and went back to history class. I do not remember his name, not a clue, but all here recorded is the truth.

✳ Presidential Nomination

Politics at that time was the paramount issue of concern. The nation was divided between Dwight D. Eisenhower and Adalai Stevenson. I was for war hero Eisenhower for my first time voting, but I had a bone to pick with him. Before my (fifth) cousin Harry left the Presidential Office, he put into place a retirement fund for retiring presidents. This was something new. Inside information was that a newly elected President would reciprocate and make it possible for Harry to not have to go back to selling hats in order to make a living. Eisenhower never did that, and Harry turned down very lucrative offers because he said they wanted the presidential office, not him.

The National Prohibition Party (NPP) was to meet in Indianapolis. I had seen lives destroyed by alcohol so I applied and was the only one to do so from California, and was appointed as the head of the California delegation with all of the floor speaker privileges.

I had seen enough booze consumed in construction camps to see better men than I am destroying their lives, and this had put me on the wagon for life. So this was a good fit.

At that time I believe the NPP was on the ballot in most states but had little or no chance of winning any national office. The convention speeches were long, dry (no pun) and cloaked in robes of pure boredom, always in a volume well enunciated by applause. A college President I had never heard of won the nomination.

I, with others, started a conga line. I was soon stopped by a reporter asking for an interview. Then I got the floor and nominated for the Presidential office a man everyone knew. This was done while ignoring the loud protests. I was hollering louder than they were.

My nomination was for a man who was converted in the Los Angeles Billy Graham Rally. This was hyped in the LA Examiner. It was Stewart Hamlin of the national radio broadcast called "The Lucky Strike Hour." He had made national news again after his conversion by his comment on the air, "If you have to smoke, smoke Lucky Strike" which got him fired.

I voted for him anyway as my first choice.

❋ On the Air

Back at school there was a barn full of things to do, but a friend and I found something unnecessary to do. We took some copper sheets, made a base, used two 6L6 tubes plus other items and made a low powered radio transmitter. The college was in a very rural area (read a vast cornfield) and I could do this and get away with it.

The call letters fell into place as all stations East of the Mississippi began with a W and the TU was a given so it was WLTU on the air. It was several months before someone asked me, "Aren't WLT your initials?" The call letters were later changed by one letter and it is the campus and government legal on-air radio station today.

A Japanese exchange student went to the away basketball games, and his recorded commentary would later be played for all the rare ones that did not go to the game. The big item was to break into a program with this: "If the young lady on the third-floor women's dorm would please pull the blind, the males over here could get some work done," followed by a quickly pulled blind.

The other factor was I went to work for RCA in Marion, Ind., 11:00 p.m. to 7:00 a.m. As an employee I could buy the latest records at the cheap, so a lot of the programming was the latest big band releases, and playing all of the requests supplied by RCA.

We had a mandatory chapel and assigned seats. I slept through the chapel service, good or bad. The seats were old wooden theater seats with fold-up bottoms. One morning, when the guy assigned to sit in front of me didn't show, I put my feet on the seat bottom. In moments, with a good footrest, I quickly dozed off.

The assigned seat holder came late and as he sat down, the whole thing acted like a guillotine on my toes. I hit a note that is still echoing in the chapel and was said to have chipped paint here and there. The speaker lost his place.

The year ended and the final day for graduation came. My parents drove from California for Ruth's and my big moment. Her parents also came and both dads wore our graduation caps. We packed and left Indiana to go to Michigan because that was where her Dad's church was, and we were to be made into one, two days after graduating.

✲ No Way to Start

My responsibility was to make a hotel reservation across the river in Canada for after the nuptials were said, which I did. The problem was, I made it for one. The desk clerk corrected me. As a new son-in-law, I had the gall to ask to borrow my new father-in-law's only car for our honeymoon, which was funded by wedding gifts of money, a whole $75.00. Fabulous it was, and yes, we went to Niagara Falls.

In the fall we had plans to go to Emory University, Candler School of Theology with a full tuition scholarship, but for now we didn't have a place to stay. A couple in Ruth's dad's church offered their house while they went away, so we moved in.

To make it more like ours, we turned over all their family pictures or put them in drawers. I worked two jobs and Ruth went back to Ma Bell where she had worked during vacations in college. I was supposed to keep the grass cut, and in Michigan it really grew.

Wouldn't you know, they came home early, the pictures still in hiding, a slat broken in the bed, and the grass not cut. I could make more money than both of us working in Michigan by going to California and working construction. We could stay in my old room behind the garage until we headed for Atlanta and seminary, so we took off.

We picked up a brand new car at the factory, to get a ride to California for driving and our paying for the gas. It was the luck of the Scottish when we got the car assigned to us. It was a factory new, hot red convertible. We drove away putting down the top and smiling like you wouldn't believe, with the sun and wind as our companions. I felt we looked like a car ad and hit the road grinning, with the pedal to the metal we were on our way.

I found my awesome bride checking out the gas gauge, and then I remembered, when I had first taken her to meet my folks, and being Scotch, (read tight) I had run out of gas on the L A freeway leaving her to flag off oncoming traffic while I walked for gas. Now she seldom lets the gas gage get below a half tank.

In the motel the next morning we both woke up with painful wind and sunburns. We never put the top down again.

❋ Summer in California

My room behind the garage with bunk beds caused my new bride to firmly say this will never do, so our making the bed had a new meaning, using a hammer and saw.

The Union sent me to a major heavy equipment contractor company and the superintendent, angry at the foreman he had just fired, asked me detailed technical questions and I knew the right answers, but never got to use them as he was still sputtering. He walked away chewing on his cigar, turned, and said I was the new foreman. Never knew a college degree had such authority.

The work was demanding, greasy, dirty, and with no excuses. The crew was up to it and no one questioned our overtime. The downside was it was night work.

Only one man on the crew gave me a problem. He was using the job as a cover to take bets, which he wrote on his thumbnail. These he could wipe off in a moment and he had never been busted. He was always broke because he was also a bet-er. He once hit eighty to one odds on a horse that hadn't stumbled coming out of the gate.

At one of our thirty minute midnight lunch breaks, he pulled out a rifle that he had gotten instead of money some loser owed on a bet. I stood up telling him to put it away, and he assured me it was not loaded, then pointed it over my head, and a lethal bit of noise and lead poked a hole in the night. I do not know which was first, his quitting or me pronouncing the crew was suddenly one man short. I was a bit shaken, but looking straight at him, he didn't need to be told the obvious.

Ruth was close to shock as I came off my first shift, job filthy. Ruth said only my eyes showed through the grease and dirt, and I was knee walking tired. I haven't a clue what she did during the day, but this event is intensely clear. We had one phone at my parent's house, and it rang, with my mother answering, "Is this Mrs. Truman?" Mom said "Yes," and the voice said, "The rabbit didn't die." Mom said, " I think you want the other Mrs. Truman."

This made it true that my Mom knew she was going to be a grandmother before we knew we were going to be chosen by God to be life co-creators called parents.

V

SEMINARY TRAINING BEGINS, EMORY UNIVERSITY

❋ Emory, Here We Come

It had never ever happened but I now had leverage: our unborn. I asked my dad for a loan to buy a car. A quick check was offered. A used 4-door Plymouth was bought, and the repayment agreed on. End of summer, we packed up and were on our way east with the car loaded to the max.

It was in west Texas late at night that we hit a storm of grasshoppers that greased the highway like snow. We stopped for coffee and I picked one grasshopper out of my coffee. Ruth stayed in the car. I still have little love for west Texas.

The biggy for me was teaching my wife how to drive our new wheels with a clutch. Suddenly engaging the clutch with the load we were carrying seemed to me to have the potential of tearing out a U Joint or putting a twist in the driveshaft before the vehicle moved. Advice: Do not ever undertake such teaching if you want to stay happily married....or even married. The old Plymouth recovered as did our love for each other, but feathering the clutch is a minefield topic.

I had a tuition scholarship for graduate studies at Emory University, in Atlanta, Georgia. Ruth had a teaching contract in nearby Decatur. But… Our best-laid plans went by the way when the principal told pregnant Ruth she would have to resign from teaching in Georgia when she began to show, so now living expenses were a consideration.

First, we had to have a place to hang our hats. When we arrived on the campus we went to a restaurant for breakfast. I ordered catfish and when my order was set down in front of me, I saw this pile of white stuff also on the plate. I did a double-take and asked, "What's that.? "

The waitress stared at me for a moment and then said, "Them's grits, you Yankee." We were truly in another world.

Our first owned dwelling, even
if it was on saw horses

❊ The Turnip Field with Potty

Married student housing was filled, so we rented a basement apartment with tiny ground-level windows that smelled musty, and everything about it was dark. There had to be something better. Enquiring at the housing office I found there was one eighteen-foot house trailer that had been auctioned off for one hundred dollars but when the bidder saw it, he turned it down. We bought it.

It had no axle, springs, or wheels. From a junkyard, I rented these. Hooking up and moving I found the frame started to come but the body didn't. The canvas roof had collapsed onto the floor and there was only a fold up couch to sleep on. We rented a spot on the edge of ten acres of a turnip field with a path to the landlord's house bathroom. I put the trailer on sawhorses, hooked up a hose, strung an electric line and we had housing.

We slept in our new home for two weeks under the stars because it took that long for me to replace the roof. We did have a white-gasoline cooking stove, and a real icebox, holding 50 lbs of ice. When it turned to winter the drain hose froze and ice melt covered the floor and refroze. Getting out of bed in the dark and being barefoot we would be instantly wide awake. When it rained the turnip field turned to mud. Chamber pot required or the boardwalk to the farm house. And this was the home to which we would bring our new child.

✳ Working in the Prison

While Ruth was teaching we stayed out of the red financially, and I could attend classes, but I knew this was short-lived and I began looking for a job. The Fulton Tower Prison ran an ad, I applied and I got a job at the prison, six days, 4:00 to 11:00 p.m. I was introduced to the ugly side of the South. While I distinctly recalled hearing that the Civil War was over, according to my history teacher, it sure wasn't here. Every staff member had honored ancestors who had fought "the blue bellies," and no one was sure where my being from California fit in.

I was to fingerprint, take the prisoner photo, and interview them. Then bind them over correctly to the county or state. I'll admit I had a problem understanding the southern dialect. Asking one woman several times about the charges against her, her answer was always "kaavan." She was arrested for carving up her husband.

One prisoner lady said she had ten children. I asked her as I typed, "Which one do you love the most?" thinking it was an impossible question. She replied, "That's easy, the one that's sick." I thought of Jesus telling the story of the shepherd who left the 99 and sought the lost sheep. Her response put in my place.

One man being booked that gave cause for me to remember him, was a street corner preacher. He must have been picked up a number of times by those who wear the badge, since all of the Deputies seemed to know him, and they were all giving him a hard time. One question hurled at him was, "When are you going to go preaching full time?" He turned, and very quietly said, looking them straight on, "When I find me a one arm usher." I was the only one who laughed.

While I am aware it certainly is not true today, but very true for the time I was a graduate student in Emory University, all drinking fountains were in twos, labeled Black and White. The men's bathroom stalls were also labeled Black and White.

What set my teeth on edge were the Civil War cannons which had been altered to have a shotgun shell inserted, then fired by every fraternity, etc, on campus. I knew that those same cannons could well have taken the lives of those who chose to preserve the United States Union and who paid the price for putting down and ending slavery.

❋ A Dinner Invitation

Strange as it is, I never went to church as a theology student any time during my first year. I planned never to give a sermon but use my skills in a way to make a difference somewhere.

Working the swing shift at the prison meant the only day I saw the sun go down was Sunday. No doubt I slept in and caught up on class assignments, maybe even studied.

The exception that happened was when a fellow student and friend, who had been appointed to thirteen churches, asked us to cover for him. He wanted me to do a church service at some rural parish he could not cover. Could we hold services?

We agreed, and arrived early Sunday morning. It was the usual one-room, white wood-framed building. I rang the church bell. This told a few that they were going to have service this Sunday. They would telephone the news to other members of the parish. I built a fire in the pot-bellied stove, swept up, set up the chairs, and rang the church bell again which said this was not a prank.

They came mostly in pickups, and they brought their family Bibles and hymnals and we had a grand time. They were appreciative as we sang, shared, laughed, taught, and brought out God's awesome good news in the scriptures.

After the service, there was an invitation to join a family for dinner. We followed a gracious family to their home, who had invited us to what I had always called lunch. The dining room table was covered with a sheet, and when removed revealed the table set for all three meals, including each family member's plate. If not washed it was at least wiped clean. We were in another world that was new to us. They, in their honest hospitality, served us an item I had never even heard about. It was boiled liver.

The rats in the cellar of my soul wanted to ask if it was shot or roadkill. I bit my tongue to not ask, but I think Ruth turned a light shade of green. Being grateful guests of this family, we both ate but passed on seconds. Ruth has never indicated she wished to fix or have boiled liver again. I should have asked if it was possum or coon but was afraid it was not.

❋ A Happening in Prison Life

One of the most savored events in prison life is when someone is released for time served. It's the envy "buzz" throughout the prison world. A prisoner was assigned to me as a man Friday. He truly was a talented guy and we worked well together. A trick he showed me was how to open a locked file cabinet, which he could do quicker than I could with the key. Everything he should not know, especially in the prison population, was in that four-drawer file cabinet. I am sure he snooped, but I had his word that he would stay out of that file. I tried to impress future secretaries by doing his trick, but I doubt I ever did impress any.

His time was served and he engaged in no long conversations. I bought a sheet cake, a few decorations and had a "going out the gate" party for him. It was by prison standards a gala party, but only office help and prison guards could attend.

He said goodby at about 11:30 or so a.m. He then took the five-finger discount at a clothing store to pick up a dress for his girlfriend before he saw her. He was arrested, and re-booked by 2:00 p.m. I hadn't taken down the decorations by that time.

My hardest thing I ever did at the tower prison was to chain up a man who was going to be executed. No need to dwell on that but it made me sick to do it.

Such was the working part of my seminary education at Candler School of Theology at Emory University.

✳ God at Work

We made it through the winter. April came as expected and Ruth without question was about to give birth. We were sightseeing with my visiting sister when Ruth's water broke and we bolted for the hospital.

Ruth was quickly taken by a nurse somewhere in no man's land while I did the paperwork. When I finished, a nurse took my trim and thin sister by the arm and started to lead her to the maternity ward. I laughed and explained, and my unmarried sister, shaking her head after a shocked silence, laughed a bit also.

The big moment of our moving into the blessed category of giving life to a brand new boy was for me a miracle. We soon bundled him up and took him home, albeit, to the trailer by the turnip field. This new life got more attention, love, or care than I thought possible. He acted like he deserved being the center of the Universe because he knew he was.

Then it happened while I held my firstborn. Projectile Vomiting. Mark just had a full bottle and this tiny baby fired all the milk across the trailer with force. A couple of days later, you could clearly see his ribs. He was starving to death.

We rushed him to the hospital and the storm of questions filled our world. God's hand in this was that the attending surgeon had lost a number of babies with the same symptoms. As an experiment, after trying all he knew, he cut through the extra muscle that had grown around the pyloric valve. This muscle was keeping the valve closed, so no milk could get through.

It was a success.This Doc was on staff and with a snip, all was solved. Our shriveled tiny baby returned to health and did demand his mother or a bottle. Mark's "NOW" meant NOW!

The other half of this story is that a fellow student who was a youth pastor, Rev. Jim Wall, had his youth group in Little Rock, AR, raise the $75.00 to pay the surgeon. I do not think I have passed up a youth car wash since.

I realized that I would never be given a student parish, being a Yankee shocked at 'Black Only' drinking fountains and toilets, etc., and troubled at the culture of those who did not know the Civil War was over. The second that I was offered a student parish in New Jersey, I took it. I transferred to Drew University Graduate School of Theology and then found that only five graduate credits can be transferred, so I was a freshman again. I received only class credits for the year at Emory.

VI

DREW UNIVERSITY SCHOOL OF THEOLOGY AND STUDENT PARISHES, ATCO AND SICKLERVILLE

❋ **Another New World: New Jersey**

We had arrived at the Millville, NJ, Methodist church, where my brother-in-law was the pastor. It was lots of hugs and no-cost board and room. Sunday, very early, my wife and I were dressed and on our way to introduce ourselves to the congregation we would be serving. We had a map and, of course, it took longer to get there than the 3/4 inches on the map indicated.

In time, there it was. A white splendor church dominated the corner. Ruth, grabbing the baby and us being late, rushed up the stairs two at a time to meet a smiling usher with an extended welcoming hand. I strongly announced that we were the newly appointed pastor and wife with a baby in arms. We were there to pastor the church. The usher's smile faded and without a word he turned and disappeared.

Soon a Priest dressed for Mass appeared and suggested

that maybe we were looking for the church around the corner. Going from glowing confidence to bewildered embarrassment and no doubt suddenly a flushed-face, it was our turn to say nothing. We quickly escaped in our old Plymouth and drove as fast as possible away from the Catholic church, around the corner to the Methodist Church.

Where it all really began, after
we found the right church

Somewhat in a state of shock, we saw an elderly plump lady standing on the sidewalk with five trays of communion cups in her arms. Never admitting what had just happened, we introduced ourselves and said some awkward words trying to cover our tardy appearance. The dear lady holding the trays turned and started for the church where a number of folk had been waiting to see what the conference had sent them this time. So far it was the new minister who needed an alarm clock.

Remember I had been booted out of my denomination, and because of working, I had never seen a Methodist service, let alone communion. How do you cover this as the lady, who turns out to be the Women's Society of Christian Service president, says "But it's World Wide Communion Sunday."

This I had never heard anything about, ever. I choked out something because I knew if I tried to bluff my way, I would be finished before I started. Thus Atco MC and our second half of the appointment, Sicklerville, were the only two churches in Christendom who did not observe Holy Communion that Sunday, because the newly appointed Methodist pastor didn't have a clue, which had to be obvious.

Later I found out why this pulpit appointment had not been filled. The former pastor had been asked to move. The newly appointed pastor had served a church where the gossip train had informed the local relatives in Atco who decided that no way was this man acceptable. I was the unknown and so we were a compromise for both sides. If I had been any greener, the cows would have rejected eating me.

The only good news in all that had happened was anything I did going forward and normal was a plus. I sure was beginning from behind the starting gate with nothing but room for improvement.

✳ The Three in One (Appointment, That Is)

A word about our other appointment on our circuit. The third church we were to serve was Tansburro MC. which was in a black neighborhood, and the three white women Trustees would not open the doors to blacks. I tried to have a service where I advertised for blacks to come and we would have dialog and make things come out right.

The blacks filled the left side of the church and no whites came, including the three who held every office in the Methodist church. The trio of white church officers kept the white-only attendance rule and I never went back.

Our second appointment was a small, country church that was easy to love, named Sicklerville. After services in the town, we would rush to our country appointment and someone on the church front steps, seeing the dust of our coming, would have the choir start in. Moments later with lots of dust in the air, I would fall in line as the choir processed. The service was always a joy.

What else than a doll house church?

To introduce myself to the community of faith, I had an evening meeting. With a smile, I said how glad we were to be in New England. The grand old man of the community, Mr. Sickler himself, stopped me cold in mid sentence. He informed me of my lack of understanding of where we were. It was not New England, but New Jersey.

He died two weeks later and my fear of exposure was front and center because I had no idea how to conduct any funeral, let alone for such an honored old-timer. I was asked if they could request a well-known pastor to do the service, and I do not know who was more relieved, them or me.

At the funeral I was quiet and tried to look officious as I stayed out of the way. Mumbling to myself, I affirmed that I was a trained ex-missionary candidate, please understand. The other issue was the date: it was the date my hero dad died, and I had my own inner thoughts and emotions to deal with. I was in the ministry way over my head.

About this time at our bigger Atco church, I had my first communion service, finding the ritual in the hymnal, but it has its special memory also. I came to the part where I was to kneel. Space was close between the altar railing and a small table where I had put the offering plates on a lower shelf. As I knelt, my knees tipped the offering plates with a crash and coins went running everywhere. I had put onto the floor all they had given.

Later in the service where I served the cup and bread, I was loudly crunching back and forth, walking on the morning offering. I had no doubts the thoughts the congregation had were not only that he has to be new at this, but he is incredibly clumsy. Is this the best the Bishop had for us?

There were very few enthusiastic handshakes at the church door as folks were leaving.

✳ Cold Coal Furnace

We were in a church board meeting when the subject came up about the coal furnace in the parsonage basement. I explained what I had done. It was to attach the vacuum hose to the blower end, build a small wood fire, added coal, and we had heat.

I must have been the idiot trying to be funny that said all you have to do is toss in a bucket of gasoline, and this was so outlandish to all of us males, it got a laugh.

Very early on Monday morning, I headed back to the

seminary leaving Ruth and baby to fend for themselves until I returned home at the end of classes on Thursday. A cold snap came along, and my wife thought it a good idea to introduce heat to the parsonage.

Ruth, overhearing (read 'listening intently'), had heard instead of the somewhat lengthy method of first building a small wood fire, then adding the coal, decided to take the quick way to heat the house, because she didn't want to leave our baby son longer than necessary. She got a bucket, and was on her way to the corner gas station to get gasoline to throw into the furnace for a quick fire start, when our nosey woman society president saw her and asked where she was going.

At the end of the week, when I returned from Drew, we had an oil-fed furnace and I still had a wife and son.

✳ Do What?

The parsonage, which was our home, was a 100-year-old building and also had been the former church. This building was now our house and home. The second floor had been added, but it truly was a fire trap.

A problem came up that I never could have envisioned, the outhouse behind the church, that few if any ever used. It was constructed by the WPA during the great depression and would have been a usable bomb shelter.

The ladies needing such, were used to using the bathroom in the parsonage and doing so during our getting ready to lead worship. I set my goal to have an indoor restroom in the church basement.

The chair of the Trustees was the widow of the head CEO of Wanamaker Department store in Philadelphia. Any bathroom change was quietly tabled or ignored. That is until I figured out what the real problem was. When I offered a double-walled (meaning soundproof) restroom, I got the ok to go ahead and build. We had privacy on Sunday morning and I was learning.

This same lady couldn't believe I could tell a bald-faced lie as I had during the children's time. I used simple magic to get the children's attention. I had a light bulb that lit up on my command (It had a battery in it and a simple switch.) No memory of the lesson now, but as with all magic, it is lies and misdirection. Her son-in-law bought the same trick and she was shocked that her pastor could speak a bold faced lie. All of which ended using magic for children's time.

Being a slow learner, in the country church we were also serving, I burned a dollar bill and made it reappear, to the same results. This truly was a never again event learned early. Some in the congregation had higher standards for a pastor than I had for myself.

✳ Sicklerville Wedding

It was in our country church that I had my first wedding. It was a wedding involving a bride named Anna Pauline Trout. What caused me to recall this wedding were her two brothers, one being named Lake and the other named Brook. This cannot be made up.

Then came my first wedding in our town church. The sanctuary was packed as they were a popular local couple. I was nervous and was trying to be cool as if I knew what I was doing.

Weddings are life affirming commitments and serious business. It had looked easy when seen from the pew, but not so when trying to think three things all at once, such as do not rush your words, speak clearly, do not mispronounce their names or go blank when right names are needed, and what was it they wanted to especially have, where in the service?

My double thoughts doubled again when I looked down and saw that I had a suit coat of different color than the trousers. Now what was it I was praying for?

Again my overworked angel came up with the answer. The bride began to cry and worked that into prize-winning sobs. Eyes wet with tears, she called out, "Has anybody got a handkerchief?" I, in my detailed preparation, did not have any except in a drawer in our bedroom. It was not the groom or me, but the Best Man who came to the rescue. Ruth attended the wedding and recalled the bride blowing her nose quite forcefully, and the ceremony resumed.

After this, the pastor's apparel was a minor issue. Ruth made me a ministerial robe, so in my haste this dress issue would never happen again. No bride ever came close to this performance in the 761 weddings that followed, but I always had a handkerchief handy, just in case.

✳ Ready to Shoot

A hair raising moment was set up by me after my midterm exams. The finals in one tough class were held in the evening in the professor's front room. He asked a question and if I had any clue to an answer at all, my hand and brain responded asap. This lasted late into the early morning, and as I was more than wide awake, I decided to go home early, since this was the last exam.

I did not want to wake Ruth or the baby, so I turned the house key as quietly as possible. I knew which step on the stair creaked and stepped past it. What saved my life was the moon light shining through a small window half way up the stairs.

In that moment Ruth saw it was me, not a thief. She was at the top of the stairs with the pistol I had been given in prison. She had my gun in her hand, and it was loaded and cocked. She was shaking, and sobbing, realizing just how close she had come to making herself a widow.

Me? I was just trying to not wake up anybody when I came home a day early.

❈ A Free Meal in the Big Apple

As intense as the studies were at the seminary, I had the good fortune to have a relationship with two incredible fellow students who taught me as much or more than I was cramming away learning in the classroom.

Chewing on ideas where real learning took place

First was my campus roomy, a WWII vet who had flown B-17s, and tried to get drunk one night to purge from his mind the women and children he was dropping bombs on. This ended up with his Christian conversion. He became a missionary in Korea and because of his military service, he became a special POW in North Korea for a mega hell-filled four years. Now he was studying to become a pastor. Larry was a Texan and each year brought with him a 100 lb. feed sack of raw peanuts,which he shared and I developed a taste for, plus a friendship of a lifetime.

The other part of our trio was Harold who was born in China to German missionary parents. He had a world view and all of the stories that go with such an education. He had proposed to his wife while they were lying in the bottom of a boat on the Yangtze River while being shot at by river pirates.

Harold had us take some time out to go into New York to a Chinese restaurant as he spoke both Manderin and Cantonese.

We took our places at the table and of course, had Harold order for us in Cantonese. The waiter looked like he was frozen, then left, and returned with the owner of the establishment. They had a short conversation in this eastern, unintelligible tongue.

The owner then stood and addressed in English the almost full restaurant, asking them to please hurry and finish, which was met with open mouthed silence. He then had the entrance door locked after the last customer left. He made a few phone calls to employees to come ASAP, then he called the staff to bring extra chairs that formed a half-circle around us. The owner explained that he wanted his staff to hear Cantonese spoken like it should be spoken.

Larry and I had a feast never to be forgotten, and Harold got in a few bites now and then. There was no check, just a forever special evening with life long friends who affected me deeply, each adding something to me to make me what I am. I believe it was their deep faith that had been tested and found to be real.

❊ Quick! Call a Painter

It was summer vacation and that meant time to do the much-needed job of painting the church. I had painted the parsonage which made the church look terrible by contrast. First a high-pressure wash job, a couple of promissory swipes of sandpaper, and plug in the paint sprayer. All went well till there was only the fifty-five-foot steeple left to paint, for which I borrowed the really tall ladders from the Atco fire department. I was painting away, enjoying the cool breeze...

BREEZE! Quickly climbing down, and sure enough, the five cars were somewhat separated, but parked at the curb down wind, and each were speckled with white paint. I took five gallons of paint thinner and washed each car and never left a note, or ever said a thing. I finished the steeple in the early dawn when there was no breeze.

Inside this wooden tower, I found a big beautiful bell on its side, cabled down in a rocker. It was rung with a rope only raising and lowering the clapper. Removing the cable that held the bell on its side, it righted and swung and sounded wonderful, which I then with joy kept ringing. Joyful that the bell was liberated and sounded great, I heard panic screaming. It was a church trustee who also was the president of the bank on the corner. He breathlessly informed me as I looked down from the bell loft that the whole tower was swaying with the bell.

Sometimes, when you do not understand why

something is done in a strange way, it's better to ask or leave it alone.

❋ A Good Idea Gone Wrong

It seemed a natural thing to do. I bought a Heath Kit for a 100-watt amplifier and put trumpet speakers in the church steeple. With a preamp and a record player playing cathedral bells, it put the church on the community map, big time. The congregation was proud of what we were giving to the village, and it was a topic of town talk.

The church was on high ground and our recorded carrilion could be heard three miles away. The steeple was so high that the sound was just right in town. Each couple of weeks I adjusted for sundown and we added to the village of Atco something unique and special. Everything was automatic and I tried to not be overly pleased with myself.

It worked wonderfully well and in my third year of studies, a married apartment opened up, so we moved, and it was back and forth to Drew during the week. Ruth got a job in Chatham teaching Home Ec. One lesson plan I knew she made was the cooking of lobster, but none ever found its way to my dinner plate.

We were back at the church on weekends. Of course, we locked the parsonage with new locks. The gift of recordings of the great carillions played each evening without us being there. I had purchased recordings by a fellow Methodist minister of Hollywood MC, Rev Charles Kendall, who had recordings playing bells that were incredible.

Then it happened. The record needle stuck in the same groove when we were not there. A hundred watts of power was proclaiming the same thing, de da, de da, de da, for several hours. I was later told this through gritted teeth. The angry neighbors (read everyone within hearing distance) had to break into the parsonage to unplug it and some folks remained hostile, saying it was maddening after a couple of hours.

Pastors have to learn to deal with hostility, not their fault, and in their prayers ask for forgiveness, even when you can hear the angels snicker.

※ Back to California

There was a lot to do leaving after three years, both in the world of academic Drew and the two churches entrusted to our care. Now it came down to the practical. I had a heavy-duty trailer hitch put on our convertible. Then I bought a flatbed trailer on which a steamroller had been transported, which seemed ideal. I built an enclosed box on the trailer bed, but I underestimated how much we had acquired. In this with everything fitted, (read, jammed, pried in), we had in one place all of our worldly goods.

The trailer was painted to match the car, the same yellow and white pattern. Folks from our town church gathered and we had prayer, tears, back-slapping, and good wishes for God giving us a safe journey. It was an emotional parting and we both were deeply moved as we began our leaving.

Pointed west and about twenty miles on our way, relaxed and savoring some of the very kind words we had spoken our way, I heard a scraping sound coming from behind. Pulling over, I found both wheels on the trailer sloped in, with the axle weld torn.

Hiring two wreckers to lift the trailer off the ground,

and two heavy-duty hubs welded to a new H steel axle, we resumed our journey, deeply grateful it did not happen on the main street of Atco with a congregation waving goodbye. To make up for the lost time I drove until just across the Mississippi River.

We were well on our way and Ruth, being a good driver and there not being a clutch to feather, took the wheel and I joined Mark asleep. Ruth encountered a rain sprinkle which made the road slippery. She topped a small hill with a sharp road turn, and the trailer, wanting to keep going straight, caused a bit of a car rear-end slide. She corrected, but the wrong way, spinning the car till we did a 180' and jackknifed.

Everything in the trailer was flung onto the wet highway and onto a muddy field. My four drawer file cabinet sent my carefully kept seminary notes fluttering in the windy rain, and U S Royal imprinted on book pages.

Oncoming traffic did not quickly stop. Our metal box 16" TV set survived but, sliding face down on the asphalt, sanded all the knobs. Clothes gathered were wet and had added weeds to their decor. Tools were flung the furthest and most were never found. Such as we could find quickly, we flung back into the trailer. As one of the wrecker crew had half said "if your trip is of God, you will have no more trouble." He must have been a prophet.

Now we were really late for the Conference in California where the church we were to be assigned was waiting and could wait no longer.

VII

UMC CALIFORNIA-ARIZONA CONFERENCE (LATER THE UMC CALIFORNIA-PACIFIC CONFERENCE)

HAVE ROBE, WILL TRAVEL

❋ **The Dreaded Conference Committee**

We were two days behind time getting to our Methodist once-a-year conference. I had been in serious written communication with Bishop Kennedy, but I was still a great unknown, on the outside trying to get in, and we absent. Looking at the map there seemed to be a shortcut through a place called Jerome, Arizona. Not a clue that it was a ghost town and a serious mountain road, but we soon found out.

The convertible we were driving was not built to pull a heavy trailer and the steam and transmission slip was real as we slowly crawled up and up, doing everything but getting out and pushing. Yes, we made it, and the only place to rest our heads when we got to the conference was the most expensive spot nearby, the Mission Inn. I am sure they considered asking us to use the back entrance, because we both were disheveled, worried, and dressed in clothes that may have been run over by trucks. We looked like street homeless.

The next morning, going quickly to where the Bishop and cabinet were meeting, I dressed in the first distressed slacks and shirt dug out of the trailer. Not being able to even find my dress shoes, I was wearing the paint-splattered moccasins I had on when I painted the parsonage and church.

First impressions are so important. I was met with silence when I walked in. It was a pastor whom I hold as a saint who broke the ice. He commented that I looked more comfortably dressed the way I was, than he felt in a tie and coat. After some interrogation, Rev. Frances Cook asked to talk to me alone, which meant this power group, who had all authority, could speak freely if I was not present. Rev. Cook and I walked slowly around the outside of the auditorium, just talking.

When we returned, he said all that needed to be said. Quietly, Rev Cook looked everyone in the eye and said, "He will do." I was mostly in for the rest of my life as a MC pastor with those three words. I had my Deacon's orders, but not my Elder's ordination, so I was put on probation. Being a stranger, I was more than happy to just be on probation.

In the years following as I shepherded those desiring to enter the MC ministry while they wrote the required papers and sweated through the required interviews, I always felt a little guilty, having been accepted with paint-splattered shoes and three words.

The bottom of the appointment list. Take it or leave it.

❋ Our First Appointment

What had been offered in back and forth letters while we were in New Jersey, was to start a new congregation with a new parsonage to live in. Since we were late and out of touch, this golden opportunity was offered by default to Kent Douglass, who became my best friend. Ruth and I went to the bottom of the appointment list, and were sent to a mountain parish with no parsonage.

My new D.S. (District Superintendent) gave me a book entitled "Dig Or Die Brother Hide" about a young Methodist minister who started a church over a saloon. Where we were assigned, oats were sold by the bushel, or drunk by the gallon, and I belonged to the Prohibition Party.

At the conference, we met the church delegation. There were five of them and they were as concerned about us as we were about them. They were great folk and we quickly became friends as we met and talked. They had questions about us and we had questions about the church.

Next was the concern of my final ordination and my

clergy robe being wadded up as roadkill in the trailer. This was set aside when I was voted to be accepted, but on a year's probation before receiving my Elder's Orders.

Knowing we were getting to the end of the list for an appointment I was almost euphoric as we met with the church delegates and I spoke of the impression they had presented. They as one corrected my mental giant-tree forest park image, by turning it into sagebrush, rocky hills, and hard scrabble living.

Conference over, we got a map to find out just where our first church to serve might be. It looked like the closest way was by Julian, a small tourist semi-mountain town, then a number of squiggly road miles further on. The map didn't exaggerate and it seemed like true wilderness as there was no evidence of civilization at all, the whole way. Ruth became very quiet as we drove down this stretch of lonely twisting mountain road.

We came to a road sign that asked us to turn right and we obeyed. At the first place we saw a fellow mortal, we asked if he knew where the Chapel Of The Hills might be? We were directed, followed by his words "It's just below road level, and looks like a septic tank." We found our new place of worship. The sign nailed to the front corner said in hand-lettered words "Methudist Church." The word Methodist was misspelled!

We were shocked to find no parsonage, but this was quickly followed by the information that a family we had never met left us the key to their place. They were on vacation and we could live there for thirty days. We met them when they returned and better people we could not imagine. We became lifelong friends.

The place the church rented for us to live in was a summer cottage built by a very short dentist, which meant there was only one room in which I could stand up straight.

The other factor? It was truly a summer cottage and one cold morning our canary froze to death. With one youngen and one in the waiting room yet to be born, being warm was a concern.

It was in the midst of the multiple demands of being a new pastor that I was jumping sideways because of everything I had to do coming at me, that wasn't getting done. Frustration meant more frustration. A couple in the congregation stood out because he was a retired Marine. No one told me this; it was obvious because he sat in the pew looking like he was at attention.

Several months down the road his wife, Ruth, came to see me. She said she just had an eye test which meant deteriorating eyesight could become blindness. She then drew a deep breath, looked at me, and said she wanted to do something worthwhile while still having her sight. Then again looking straight at me, said she wanted to be my secretary as I sure needed a good one! Then with a smile added that she was volunteering.

Recovering from this minor miracle, we agreed, and life took on a whole different dimension. She was a God sent answer and became the multitasker I desperately needed. She was all I could hope for and I am happy to report that she had her eyesight till God called this saint to join the others in eternity.

✳ Tragedy Opens a Door

It happened too often. There was a car accident on this twisted mountain road and I happened to be first on the scene. I held the bloody head of the only survivor on my lap. It took an hour for the ambulance to come, and an hour to get back to the hospital. I never knew if he made it or not. What I did know was I had to get an ambulance.

I found one but it needed a major overhaul. With what I had learned in my teens, I overhauled it, but with modifications. It now could outrun anything on the mountain.

The first call was for an overturned WWII jeep with the weight of the jeep edge resting across a twelve-year-old head. He wasn't wearing a helmet or a seat belt and he didn't need an ambulance.

I learned I had to have help. I asked for volunteers. Those who heard the firehouse siren make short multiple blasts, the willing would meet me by flagging me down on my way to the highway. The surprise was when a truck would lose its brakes and be out of control, the driver would lay on its air horn on the way past our village. I could be on my way and picking up help before the accident happened.

For a truck without brakes, it was a sure thing that at Horseshoe Curve a truck wreck was waiting patiently to happen. When we got there the dust had not started to settle but the truck driver was a pro. He had run the truck up on the bank and laid it on its side. The good news was he was not hurt and the other good news was the truck was filled with frozen chicken. I didn't ask but he shrugged his shoulders and said why didn't I take the chickens? We did until there wasn't room for one more. Frost was forming on the inside of the ambulance and I was thinking of all the ways we could pass along such a gift back home. We had shaken hands and were in the cab departing with fried chicken on our minds when...

I didn't see it happen, but two elderly seniors looking at the carnage and not the road, drove over the edge and rolled down the canyon. I heard the crunch of metal as it was misshapen by its complaining about the rocks. Getting down to what once was a car, I found the man outside across the hood and his wife inside wide-eyed and in a state of shock. We had a lot of help from people who stopped to get them back up to the road and on the gurney. We had lots and lots of help unloading the chickens.

Then it was red lights, siren and pedal to the metal all the way to the hospital. Frost was still on most of the insides as seen in the rear view mirror. This gave us the only complaint that any of our wounded passengers ever lodged: " It was such a cold trip down the mountain."

On the way back up the mountain, there was not one frozen chicken left and this couple never paid the dollar a mile I billed them for their ride.

Because I knew how to build a stroker (hot mill-motor), I attracted the stray teen males of the parish. I dubbed them the "Bishop Riders", and they pledged to give roadside help when needed. The girls were recruited to work in the basement church. I had taken a closet for my office but it needed painting. One early teen distinguished herself by stepping into a bucket of paint. That was not so bad but she then ran. Ponder that for a moment and think about clean-up.

I remember her vividly because later she came into my study shaking and teary-eyed. It is hard to forget her words: "Dad is drunk and says he is going to kill Mom and me." I hunted him down, with her help. He was a torpedo man, First Class, on leave from the U.S. Navy. He was easy to spot in our local watering hole, liquored up and irrational with the booze doing most of the talking. With the barkeep's help we got him to a storage room and I left when he was asleep.

His wife, with knives in her eyes, asked me about her getting a divorce, then asking me what she should do every other sentence. I never saw this sailor again but I knew his marriage was over and his daughter was deeply scared where it doesn't show, but is raw and real. The family moved and I never knew where. Such is the backside of life in a mountain parish.

❋ The Unexpected

Out calling, I seemed to always find someone doing something I didn't expect. Up a dead-end road was a shack and a man inside who was using a linotype. He wrote stories for cowboy westerns and got the princely sum of ten cents a word. His comment was that if there was a gunfight, no cowboy died with just one shot, and most often it took all six shots to do the deed. I was impressed with anyone who had such a command of the English language that he could set the type for the printer and not make a spelling error.

Then there is what I never understood, then or now. Remember this was hill country and at times I got to make my calls on skis, always a joy. I had heard of a hilltop ranch, with a top of the world view. I didn't know the people but I asked them for permission to have a hilltop Easter Sunrise service on their property. Being on a hilltop it would be blown clean of any snow. I asked and they said it would be no problem, but there was limited parking. The whereabouts of the Easter Sunrise service was put on the church calendar.

We had a few snow flurries but nothing serious untill Easter Sunday morning. A major cloud burst storm arrived overnight and dumped so much snow that a hilltop service was out of the question. A handful of the faithful did gather at the church for the Easter sunrise service because none of the roads were ever plowed. Later the sheriffs came asking a lot of questions and answering none.

It was the next day I was told the lady who owned the property had been murdered during the night. You now know as much as I did then about anything to do with this tragedy because I was told to keep my nose out of it by the rude man with a big badge.

✳ Don't Do This at Home

It is a simple law of physics. Near the surface of the earth, all objects fall 32 feet in the first second and 64 feet in the next second, etc. Knowing this, I would put a silver dollar on the back of my outstretched level right hand, and wax bullets in my 38 cal. The pistol knew exactly where that coin would be when dropped from the same height every time. Practicing doing this fast draw, I could put the wax bullet on the coin almost every time. It was fast, noisy, and impressive.

A dead-end canyon was behind our house and I used it for target shooting. It was a short blind canyon, and perfect with no neighbors. A telephone repairman came up the hill as I was practicing with my 22 caliber target rifle on a flyspeck target. He was a gun buff, so with a common interest, we traded stories and as with most males, we tried to top each other's story.

To show off, I got my 38 handgun, given to me by a prisoner while working at the prison in Atlanta. I did the fast draw trick that I had practiced. He was impressed, then after a bit he repaired whatever was wrong with our phone. He left and we parted as newfound friends.

Later that evening, I was told that when he finished his shift, he took his pistol and tried this trick at home, since it looked so easy. His first fast draw, he put a bullet through his right foot. I have never demonstrated that trick again from that day to this. Please do not try this trick; I have enough guilt.

✳ Don't Play with Fire

Our mountain parish had lavish scenery -- but only a fireplace for heat. This was critical with a newborn. I visited the Ranger office often to get a permit to fall dead trees for the voracious appetite of our fireplace. I would fell the tree, and then cut it into fireplace lengths, while Ruth gathered and carried the wood to the trailer.

Encountering a telephone crew I saw a shortcut to an abundant wood supply. I asked the phone guys for the poles they were replacing, and pushing my luck, asked if they would take the poles to the top of the hill where we lived, and they did. Cutting my winter warmth blessings with my chain saw and then splitting it with an ax was hard work, but the wood stack was bigger each day and made me feel good knowing it would keep us warm on snow days.

With little ceremony, I lit off a fire from our new woodpile in our fireplace, It being a cool evening. You guessed it. Black clouds of choking smoke rolled out of the fireplace, filling the front room, then the whole house. Ruth grabbed our toddler and ran outside and I was close behind. It took buckets of water to stop this greasy creosote fire which laid a blanket of smudge over all the windows, beds, and us.

Any fool knew this would happen, and I suddenly stood at the head of that line. No, I never shared this story with any member of the congregation, my dad or anyone else.

Not to be outdone, I offered a trailer load of fine aged firewood to my boss, the District Superintendent, as I knew he had a fireplace. No, I did not include any telephone pole wood. I learn slowly but good. I delivered cut dead forest trees, stacked it, and accepted his thanks for my thoughtful gift. Later he asked me what were all of those white bugs that were flying out of his fireplace? Some days you just can't win.

❊ The Family Grows

Our future member of the family was making his/her demands known as Ruth took my hand and asked if I felt that kick. This had to be a future field kicker for the LA Rams! What I wanted for this child was a first class ride in the church ambulance down to the hospital. This meant putting it in first class shape. I had almost gotten a ticket on my last ambulance run. The cause was the siren growling going through town because the brake in it needed tightening. How did I know?

I was stopped again by the highway patrol officer who, being cruel of heart, started to write me a ticket. I stuck a pencil in the blades of the siren and said "Fixed". He tore up the ticket. Back up the mountain I knew such thinking would lead to a tune-up which ended by my doing a valve grind. No reason to hurry, as at Ruth's last visit the Doctor smiled and guaranteed a late date of birth, so the ambulance engine head sat on the workbench.

It was New Years Eve, and I had set up a family church service event from 8:00 to 12:00 p.m. to say so-long to the old year and welcome the new. It was food the first hour, lots of games with kids aplenty in the middle, and more adults than I expected for the last hour. It was about that time for the worship service to begin, when the phone rang. I was told it was my wife calling. She said to come home NOW!

Shocked at what she meant, I made tracks home, put Ruth in the Plymouth and headed down the mountain, flat out, meaning post haste, only to have her tell me to turn around to go to the doctor's office two miles up the mountain. Her water broke on the doc's doorstep, and then we turned around again and went down the mountain, a forty-eight mile trip.

Rebecca Joy made her entrance to this life a few moments after midnight, but missed by a hair being the first born in San Diego County and a college scholarship. I got my picture in the paper with Becky, but not Ruth. Meantime I had forgotten the gathering at the church service where people waited for news and waited and waited, then went home fearing the worst. But they were wrong.

Our daughter fulfilled her grandmother's prediction: a beautiful, blue eyed, redheaded, freckle faced addition to the family. She wrapped me around her finger, and I'm still not loose.

✳ Trying to do the Right Thing and...

This is a confession that I truly am a slow learner. The conference offered sponsorship of couples from Indonesia to any MC who signed up. I signed up. The husband had been in a Japanese concentration camp and had training as an architect. This was going to be a great adventure.

Most of the community helped as we gathered furniture, cooking pots and pans, and all else to set up housekeeping in the hills. Remember, this part of the world was one step from poverty, so all things given were usable, but a bit shop-worn.

The greatest majority from the church and some of the community went with us to the airport to greet and welcome our refugee couple. Believe me, there was electric excitement in the air and anxious expectation. The Women's Society of Christian Service president was dressed in her best gingham, covered by a sweater with holes at the elbows. She was excited and front and center in all of this.

Then the shock. The refugee couple descended down the stairs of the plane and the wife took the show. She was dressed as though she was going to "Hollee-wood," pencil line watch, 4" high heels, fur coat, and we all stood with our mouths open, staring. No one said or could say a word.

It went downhill from there. The husband had architectural training; I got him a job as a draftsman. Because he only had experience with the metric system he lasted only two weeks.

On the home front, I got a call to come quickly to a parishioner's home. I rushed over and was greeted with the caller handing me a really big pair of Navy binoculars. I was told to look. Sure enough, with the magnification worthy of stargazing, there was our refugee wife across the valley. I found myself looking at our "relaxed" wife sunning herself and beyond a doubt, she was shockingly "not overly dressed."

I got to take them through the first large grocery store they had ever seen and listened to them exclaim, as we walked past the many over-full shelves, heavy with food and the wonder of it all. It was the same as we went through each department of the store. All of which made me ponder long and deep about my blessing of being born here in the U.S.

They were not ungrateful. They had been performers somewhere in their past and they offered to do their thing to pay back the church for all we had done. I booked the social hall of our rather large MC in La Mesa, pulled in a favor and got the lighting and sound equipment belonging to the recreation center of San Diego, rented chairs, then notified all the San Diego Methodist churches of what we were doing and offering.

Six people showed up. The pastor of the La Mesa Church, his wife, the District Superintendent, and his wife, Ruth, and myself.

The couple soon mentioned trying out living in Hollywood. What she said to her husband when she saw the empty cavern of the auditorium left no doubt that this was their next step. I do not know if they shook the mountain dust from their feet, but they were gone.

So ended our help, trying to do a good thing.

✳ Going to Prison Again

Everyone checked them out. It was a small, mountain close-knit community and these folks showing up for church gave life to quiet nattering among the observant. The new couple were in their late middle earlies and had driven 30 miles in order to attend worship service in our Chapel Of The Hills, an elegant name for what one citizen described as a septic tank down the hill.

They were the new Prison Warden and his wife from down by the border. This made me pull up my theological socks. If someone was going to come that far to attend services while some folk wouldn't walk across the street to do so, I had to really buckle down on sermon preparation.

He soon asked me to be the Prison Chaplain at an

extension of Chino Institute For Men, so now, on my day off, I was driving sixty miles weekly for my extra job. I found I had complete freedom at this Graybar Hotel with no one to tell me what I could and could not do.

Being a Psych major I divided "the guests" who were willing, into four groups. First was psychological tests as tools for self-awareness, etc. The second was Bible study as an awareness of the purpose of life and inner spiritual help found in Scripture. Third, was talk therapy, self-discovery where I only said "Hmmm" a lot and looked wise, but without a pipe. My last control group, I did nothing. The purpose was to see which group had the fewest guests returning to prison, since recidivism was a major issue at the time.

Soon after, being appointed to a city church, I did not gather enough data to know the effectiveness of any one group. I did refer all of this study to Sacramento if they would like to extend the study. They offered me a full-time job which I turned down.

What happened on my last visit to this prison was for the guards a mystery. One group gave me a beautiful hand-done copy of the 23rd Psalm framed under glass. The mystery was that a small windowpane was missing and there was no broken glass anywhere. Shards of glass are a deadly weapon and no prisoner would clean up splinters of broken glass without being told to do so. My gift had glass in the handmade simple wooden frame. It was truly a trophy gift and a life keeper.

The other gift was a framed piece of copper where a prisoner had saved the wooden tongue depressors and on the cement floor of his cell, had shaped them into tools. From the hobby shop he obtained a sheet of copper. He then pressed into the reverse side the picture of The Last Supper, which hangs now in our back room.

Checking out of this State free housing to go home, I overheard two of the guards talking about their concern over the missing glass mystery. I happened to have both gifts under my coat and didn't bother interrupting their thoughts.

While I was serving another church some years later, someone used the five-finger discount to take this prison gift of the 23rd Psalm, or it grew legs.

✳ A Special Funeral

He was bright, always underfoot, had more questions than I had answers, and he was twelve years old, I missed him for a couple of days, and his folks told me he was in the hospital and he had asked for me. I visited the hospital. When I left he said, "See you in the morning, Rev."

He died on the operating table later that day from a brain tumor. I had the funeral, but the burial spot was on a hill way off the beaten path or any other path. The hearse spun its wheels on the steep dirt slope, and I with my battered yellow convertible, now with truck tires and a log chain, got in front of the funeral coach and together we made the grade.

It was an old Indian burial ground. I could see that hilltop from highway 80, and each time I passed, I knew I would meet, at some time of God's own choosing, a plucky twelve-year-old with lots of questions on that great gettin-up morning, and I will have some of my own to ask our Creator.

A promise was given to us by the One back from the dead who said, "Because I live, you will live also." The boy's memory and his funeral are still very real.

❋ The Switch

He could almost hold his own with a sumo wrestler; he carried a few extra lbs. How we attracted him I have no idea, but it had to be the event of divine origin. I quickly hired him at fifteen dollars a week. Gifted musicians are rare and he was classically trained and this was where his heart was. He became our church pianist.

He earned his bread playing for a night club until two in the morning, then driving the twisting mountain roads, sleeping in his car till time for church. Consider this, while playing a classical piece, the piano stool split under him -- and he didn't miss a note as he stood up to finish. For a small church meeting in a basement, we had a first-class music program.

I put him behind a "rude" screen up front where he could not be seen. He had a hot pot of coffee, enjoying the heavenly elixir, and the congregation could enjoy only the tantalizing smell. It kept both awake. He sat where I could just see him and he would shake his head no when we differed, since he was an Episcopalian and I was a half baked Methodist.

Again I built an amplifier and put a speaker high in a tall pine tree, sending evensong bells out over the community. Also, it served for sound when needed in the service, controlled by a switch. One morning our staff musician accidentally switched it so the sermon went out of the pine tree speaker. An American Indian was sitting still on a mountain ledge waiting with "old meat in the pot" (his rifle) for a deer to wander into range. While waiting, he said he heard God talking to him in the canyon. He soon figured it out, and came and saw me.

I had his baptism in a swimming pool some twenty miles away in Julian, and made a great member and a friend of faith led by God's own purpose by a mistaken flip of a switch.

✳ The Wedding

Having not a clue then or now, how or why, I had been asked to do a fashionable wedding while serving a nowhere mountain, obscure parish.

The wedding was to be held in beautiful Balboa Park. The date and time were upon me. I got ready to go. My helpmate wife was my in-resident barber. My hairstyle was a flat top. She used an electric set of clippers and with a rock-steady hand, she always did a professional job. Besides, there were no barbershops in any direction.

Sitting still as instructed, Ruth was about half-finished when the clippers gave up the ghost, followed by her exclaiming, "Oh, NO!" This was a semi-panic time till I recalled that one of our church members had mentioned to me he had been a Navy barber. Donning my best (and only) suit, grabbing my homemade robe, and the book of rituals of the Methodist Church, I made record time getting to my friend's house. Yes, he still had clippers and had done hundreds of flat tops. Time was getting short so do I tell him to hurry or let him do a good job? He did both.

His wife, a late sleeper, got up and offered me a cup of coffee which was gratefully welcomed. She then withdrew an enema bag from her bed and poured me a cup of lukewarm coffee from that red bag, commenting it kept her feet warm at night and she could have her first cup in bed in the morning.

Down the two-lane, twisting, winding, mountain road I went, full bore. Having driven the ambulance service we had set up, I knew the road. Of course, being late was inexcusable. When I got to the flat land, it was floorboard driving. I was waved over to the side of the road by a highway patrol cop. It seems I had not noticed the motorcycle policeman somewhere along the way, as I had eyes only for the road.

This patrolman had radioed ahead to stop me, his story being that he could not get his bike started, or I later wondered if he could not catch me since I had some good stuff under the hood.

One point I learned from this: never ever say to a policeman "Hurry up." I did ask to have him follow me, let me do the wedding, then take me to jail. He never even looked up from what he was writing in his book. He had me get out of the car, hands on the car, and when he saw my clerical robe and ritual book, Holy providence entered the picture because he lectured me and I did NOT get a rightfully, well-earned ticket.

I hit the throttle hard as I was now really late. This threw dirt and gravel at his patrol car and I cringed. He followed me for a bit and I seriously doubt he was smiling. I got to the Bowl in the park, found a parking place, took a deep breath, but still knew the whole wedding party was checking their watches.

All of the massive decorations were done in pink. All of the bridesmaids were in pink down to the flower girl who was in a pink dress, socks, and shoes. They each carried a pink bouquet of flowers. The ring bearer was dressed in a pink tux. The groomsmen were all wearing pink tux and you guessed it, all the men had a pink carnation in their lapel. I did not know there were so many flowers that were pink or where they found a pink carpet for the bride and guests to walk on.

My clerical robe was black and I only looked pink. Not a word was said about my bad timing as everything was on hold. In fact, the bride's mother said, "Thank God the minister is on time!" Her watch had to be slow. It seems the soloist, the star of the Starlite Opera Company, had not arrived. An hour later she finally came and we began the ceremony. She had the time wrong on her calendar.

After the wedding the couple left in a brand new Cadillac convertible; pink, of course. I would note that the Cadillac emitted pink smoke but that would not be true. They missed that opportunity.

I drove back up the mountain carefully observing the speed limit. I also stopped at the home of my emergency barber to thank my friend for the hurried half hair cut. I was not offered any more coffee out of the red rubber cafe. Life returned to normal.

✳ **Mountain Culture?**

Calling on an unfamiliar cabin, the lady of the house called out from the porch "NO FURTHER." I, being still in motion, she fired a shot to my right.Then and there I decided not to make a pastoral call after all. These mountain folk had their reasons to be private, mostly, it was not the government's business what you did. I took another step and was thankful that she was a good shot, was sober and she had declared with full voice and her 30-30 rifle spoke loud and convincingly, that I was not welcome. I figured that smarts said turn around and get gone. In my calling book, I marked it as not welcome, with an exclamation point.

Another encounter happened the first week I was the pastor. A gruff older woman with a wooden leg confronted me. I never recovered fast enough to ask her name after she said her piece. The gossip said she was an ex-military retired Major. She did speak with the authority of a 30 year top Sergeant voice and did so to me with these words: "If I ever catch you crawling out of a bedroom window, I will kill you!"

I was struck dumb and never heard another word spoken to me by her in the years that followed. The week we were leaving for our next church she handed me an unabridged dictionary, again without a word. It is a gift I still have. I took it that I had passed her test for keeping on living. The big X factor was, I was very happily married and wanted to stay that way.

It was a life changing moment when Ruth casually mentioned that she knew another member was going to join our family. My first thought was, which cousin is going to mooch off of us? She was silent for a moment, then what she meant slammed into me. It was an instance of half dropping to my knees, or jumping up and shouting. There are no words for such a revelation and this time, I didn't care which kind, boy or girl, it was joyful happy news.

Things were normal till Ruth's time was close and I had the bad taste and timing to be put in the hospital with infected kidneys, with the doctor saying it could be fatal if I did not slow down. I was twenty-nine years old.

My deal with Ruth was she would name the boys and I the girls. Timothy was sent home with a once a month need for a gamma globulin shot at $40 each, and we were earning three thousand dollars a year! He was allergic to most everything on the mountain. When we moved to the city, he never had another shot because he thrived on the foul traffic air of city living.

Our pooch, Danny, always accompanied Mark to the bus stop, then with our son safely on his way, he ran to meet Mark as he got off the bus at school. Our pet distinguished himself by being awarded a Perfect Attendance Certificate at the grammar school graduation. We all missed that loyal faithfulness wrapped in black fur, with a cold nose, a fast tail wag and face lick greeting. Sorry that we felt we had to adopt him out instead of moving him with us into the big bad world of the city.

VIII

OUR CITY MINISTRY BEGINS

A new world to us. The city.

⁂ The City Beckons

Our world was upended big time.

Moving is a bad word not used in mixed company. But where were we to move? The L. A. Times printed all of the moves of the Methodist Clergy which had been confirmed by the Bishop at the annual conference. After we knew for sure we were moving, we in a heartbeat were off to see our new appointment. There it was, a derelict building suffering from lack of any care, with graffiti, some even being religious, painted or smeared on the outside, but not on the inside. This appointment would put tears in the eyes of a wooden statue. It sure did in mine. The septic tank church, all of a sudden, looked pretty good.

I had just come from being the speaker at a high school week-long retreat and felt really good about how things went, with the camp nurse saying she wanted me to be the pastor of her church. Now Ruth and I were in shock.

Sick of heart we quickly found the District Superintendent again at the conference and scared, asked if this appointment was final, or if there was any other choice?

He said yes, there was one. I do not recall if we went to see this offer or accepted it on the spot. It turned out to be a newer plant with no graffiti. The story soon emerged that a former pastor's kids had started a fire that took the former church which had stood there for some sixty years. I have to admit that I was quietly very grateful to some PKs (Preacher's Kids) who had played with matches.

We were city folk now and we adjusted quickly. The in-resident saint, who lived on the other side of the church and held the church together, now watched our three youngsters race up and down the sidewalk. She then quietly commented,"Where you came from you didn't have sidewalks." She was sure right.

The parsonage was sandwiched between the sanctuary and the parking lot. A parishioner on the church porch was only feet from any window on that side of the parsonage, and we were often greeted through our bedroom windows. Besides that, the choir rehearsed in our front room on Sunday morning. It had a new snow-white rug newly installed for us. It was a rug that Ruth scrubbed on her knees every Saturday night.

When we needed more Sunday school rooms, we offered one of our children's bedrooms. One trustee said,

"No thanks. I would not put our daughter in that fire trap."
And our children lived there!

Fire did appear once behind the water heater in the
dryer lint and Ruth hesitated before putting it out. Her
thoughts were, "If I grab the children, we'd have time..."
She chose to put out the fire.

✳ Our Kids and the City

The city was a new world for our brood, and they took full
advantage of all the freedom it offered. Tim was in robust
health. Seems he was allergic to mesquite and clean air.
In the city of smog and gas fumes from city traffic, he
blossomed.

So one day, while Ruth was at the doctor and I was
dressing Becky, he took off on his tricycle, crossing
several major intersections and we had no trail of cookie
crumbs to find which way he had gone. The hand of God
intervened, as Tim hadn't a clue what a red light meant, or
what a crosswalk was for, but he was bent on seeing it all.
An unknown saint brought him back covered with melted
chocolate ice cream, and how she knew where he lived
was never known.

Mark, our firstborn, was nine and had been warned
of all the dangers of the city we could think of, without
scaring him. He was coming home from school and as
instructed, waited for a green light before crossing a major
boulevard. Stepping off the curb into a crosswalk as he
was told, a car running a red light hit him and flung him
some distance.

No recall how I was informed of this, but I was quick
enough to go and pick up our son out of the street and
carry him to the curb. The ambulance soon came, and

we went to the hospital together. Holding my scraped, traumatized son, the good news at the hospital was that it was just a broken leg. He healed quickly but I added to his city instruction, "Look both ways." The driver's lawyer asked us to drop charges because I was clergy. We didn't.

Becky, at four, did things in her own style as always. She decided to disrobe while sitting on the parsonage front steps. Not sure if she was protesting all of the kids who came for Sunday School and ended up playing with, and scattering and breaking her toys? She had been quite vocal on this issue, since some strange girl had taken a liking to her favorite doll.

❋ Playing to Win

There were five Methodist churches in town and I was now pastor of "St. Fifth by the Wash" (LA river). Dealing with being number five in size, I noted there was a volleyball league between the five UM churches. I quickly joined up. Joyfully busy beyond description and with no time to build a team, I asked a young man to do this for the church. He was waiting to join the military. We soon were an up and coming force in league play.

This gifted and talented young man, while seated on the couch in our front room, accepted Jesus into his life. To affirm his decision he gave me his 45 caliber army pistol. He went on to attend seminary and after his ordination served several churches in our conference.

I had a few things published in the local paper, was appointed to the Library Building Board by the Mayor, and joined the Optimist service club, becoming in time the State Chaplain. All of this led to my being nominated for Young Man of the Year.

My challenging work was lecturing on the book of "Job" for the University Women.

I was hired through Chino prison to be Chaplain to the men in prison camp #37 up by Mt. Wilson. This meant rain or shine, I went up the mountain to 20 miles beyond Mt. Wilson, and my proud achievement there was to establish a library. I was busy.

My sadness was that I tried to play God. One of the prisoners was an incredible woodcarver artist. Having a friend who was a curator of an art studio in New York, I shipped the prisoner's best pieces to him and they sold quickly for New York prices. I felt he was an incredibly outstanding talent and went to bat for him to be released, at least on probation. In a short time because of this, he was a free man on his way to a good life.

Four months later he died of an overdose of drugs. It was painful to know that I had not figured this into what I meant for good. There was nothing I could do to bring him back except live with what I had done. Every once in a while this comes to mind and it reminds me to not ever play God.

We remodeled some of the church, especially the entrance to the sanctuary which upgraded the looks of the whole. It was not all a bed of roses but it did have a few bare stems and a few thorns.

One layman held five chairmanships in the church: administrative board, Trustees, Finance, Social Concerns, and was Head Usher. He would take the ushers out when the sermon was to begin, and they would sit on the back steps till they heard the organ play for the closing hymn. My response was to start using more humor in the sermon. The ushers would come in to find out what the laughter was all about. I do not feel that being a stand-up comedian is right for the pulpit, but it got the ushers back in church.

The Trustees' chairman continued to warm the back steps alone.

At this point of life in the parish, I was asked by the Conference to take four college men to Africa to teach the care and use of some 462 one-cylinder diesel tractors. These were a gift from the area churches to the Congolese people as they received their freedom from Belgium. That and the revolution that followed is a story by itself.

❉ Celebrating a Life Milepost

With the blessing of the church, our lives changed again: I went to Africa and Ruth and our three children went to Michigan to spend the summer with her parents. The young man mentioned above took over the church for the summer, and we were off and running. I still have the front-page headline in my life scrapbook, printed in red ink, as a reminder: "MINISTER MISSING IN CONGO."

For the full Africa story, turn to the second part of this book. Suffice it to say we all survived, came back, and took up where we left off. Ten months later our fourth son Nathan was born....while I was at a meeting.

It was our tenth wedding anniversary, and Ruth was healing from surgery. While recovering, the diamond had dropped out of her engagement ring onto the blankets. She found it and gave it to me to be reset, but I had another idea.

We both wanted to celebrate our tenth anniversary. This called for our having a special dinner. Just before we left, I placed a diamond pendant around her neck -- what had been her engagement ring -- and she burst into tears, stammering that now she couldn't see her ring. Consoling her as best I could, we left for our anniversary dinner.

This was a personal moment. The place I chose was a dimly lit Italian restaurant and I had a coupon (of course). The shelf behind the booth where we were led to sit was covered with wine bottles which added to the ambience. Our conversation turned to this unique wall dressing. I reached back and picked up one bottle, turned it over to show my ten year bride that it was empty, and it wasn't.

There is something about a pastor smelling like a brewery, that causes a prayer to be quickly uttered that no parishioner had seen this accident. Nothing to do but quickly look around, and sit low while wiping up the embarrassment from both of us.

We were late, having not planned enough time, so without the dessert that came with the meal we left for Grauman's Chinese Theater. The new film playing was Westside Story.

I had a ten dollar check from a wedding which I had saved for this special evening, thinking the theater would accept it or cash it. Maybe it was the wine aroma we both brought with us, but something brought a flat NO to cash it or pay our way in. Nobody else would cash the check! We did not see the film.

Going to Bob's Big Boy for our missed dessert and while eating ice cream, I took from my wallet something I had planned for this evening. I tossed a wad of toilet paper on the table. She asked me what this was. It was a new engagement ring with a stone you could see. She hugged me, said she loved me and the ring. She has worn it since. The home turf was at peace again.

Not long after that we moved.

IX

A JOYOUS APPOINTMENT

❋ Build, Build, Build

The move we were offered this time was more than we could ever hope for. Having heard about the community, it seemed a bit of O'Henry, or unreal. The story was that it had once been a very elite Country Club, centered around a horse racing track. A man of a different ethnic order applied for membership in the Country Club and was turned down. Instead of accepting this rejection, he quietly went about buying it all.

As the new owner, he announced he was going to subdivide the property. How the church got the prime piece of property is unknown to me. However, this piece of ground did come with a headstone for "Beatrice" and "My Girl". Noted on the headstone: "Horses who gave their all at Midwick Country Club." This headstone for the two racehorses disappeared, but was found in a bar and returned.

The folk who moved into the development were all about the same age as we were and we were all raising families, so church growth was to be had. The biggest problem for us was that the parsonage only had two bedrooms and we had three sons and a daughter. The upside was that there was a rose garden in the front yard to enjoy, so we managed. It was a grand and wonderful place to live.

Church came first which meant building Sunday school rooms, a first class play yard with all plants of the Holy Land, a social hall with a first-class kitchen. We made a big deal dedicating this exciting unit with every church dignitary called to participate who I could think should be at the dedication.They all came.

Of course, I wore my clerical collar and it was a big affair. But I had a personal conflict. I had signed up to compete in a race called a trollum at Riverside Race Course, driving an MG-B in class. I knew I could do well. I had rebuilt it to do well.

All of the dignitary speakers talked too long at the dedication. My mind was on the race and I knew I would have to compete way out of class.

When I got to the starting line, I saw in the lane beside me a Corvette and a young lady at the wheel. I put on my helmet and my flame-retardant suit over my cleric, but my clergy collar was showing. Just before the bottom light turned green, she glanced over, and saw my clerical collar. Her jaw dropped looking at me and at that same moment I had a green light. I came off the line with my four cylinders wound tight, turning six grand. She never caught me. It went into the books, "MG-B had a better time than a Corvette" in the sharp turns of the trollum.

Unthinkable. I wanted to hug my wonderful MG-B.

✳ One More Car Story

On another day, at the bottom of our hill, a car was stopped in the middle of the street. A man was berating it with his classic curse words, rage, and pounding it with his fists. Of course, I asked him if it was for sale? No surprise, it was. He agreed with my first offer, fifty dollars. I now owned a French Renault Dauphine with a Ferlack Electric clutch. I soon found I may have paid too much. Every time I worked on it, I knew why France lost the war.

❋ A Real Carillon

Because the church sat on high ground, I proposed a carillon (set of bells) on a tower. A member architect designed a floating platform that met the city's concern over earthquakes. Another member had saved every Vatican stamp issued. This collection at auction met all costs. The city raised the issue of the tower being too tall. With a time capsule buried in the top and a blinking small red light, we got our building permit.

It is shown in the book of things worth seeing in Los Angeles. This was because the company that made the bell stanchion which held the beautiful fiberglass bells, (with speakers inside), did a fantastic job and took pride in what they made.

I was as happy as a clam in deep water. Busy time.

❋ Whitney Portals: Never Again

One of the joys of working hard was to go where there are no phones, and for us on minimum salary and four "rugrats" (this was the term most commonly used at that time by tent campers), meant borrowing the umbrella tent from my parents. We alternated between the west and east sides of the Sierras, but always camped in the glory of the high country.

We loved the place called Whitney Portals, which made it the go to place to camp. It was ideal. The scenery was all our eyes could wish for. Becky spotted our past campsite and we quickly set up camp. The tent stakes were hammered down on the familiar level site. It was backed up to a mountain stream that serenaded us around the clock. At the head of this narrow canyon was a medium shallow pond which was stocked once a week with eight inch rainbow trout for children to fish for. Drowning worms on a hook only bothered Becky. There was a shack store which had most things we needed or forgot.

The best thing was after all were in their sleeping bags, I hung a Coleman lantern behind a camp chair and caught up on my reading. I now realize why Ruth seemed to be tired, cooking, kid watching, dishes, which I may have helped with less than I can now claim.

It was dusk, fast turning to dark. Campfires were ablaze and s'mores and marshmallows, burned or ablaze, were to follow. A Scoutmaster came to our campsite and asked me to join a search party for a lost four year old. The last he was seen was by his two siblings with him on a bridge over the creek. A valley search began with lanterns and flashlights among the rocks. Quickly all males were enlisted, joined up by the pond-lake, and lined up. We moved together down the valley, shoulder to shoulder, looking behind every bush.

Many hours later, tired and with leg wounds picked up from stumbling in the dark, searching behind every boulder, tree, and opening up every shadow, we gave up. Our tent was dark and as I undressed, I heard Ruth say she had heard a voice tell her that the child was under a log in the creek behind camp nineteen. What can I say but that spooked me because that was not like Ruth.

The next morning the scout leaders pulled the body out of the creek and laid it on our table. Someone said they had recovered the body under a log behind camp nine above us. We packed and left and have never returned.

✳ Hysterical Bride

There are times when a couple asked to be married and as we got acquainted and into counseling, it became evident that they did not really know each other or maybe should not consider marriage. At least not without some serious counseling. This seldom happened, but did often enough to be noted.

You cannot tell a couple this because they are not aware of what I picked up in our exchange in the conversation. If I tell them, they will leave and get married around the corner. When it was evident they truly did not know each other, I used several methods of letting them come to that conclusion and discover this for themselves. This is subtle but it works and can prevent a lot of pain and sadness in their future.

Just before I would go out at a wedding to begin my pre-wedding piece, I asked in private, both the groom and the bride, if they wanted to go through with the wedding. Never had a groom say "no", but two brides did. This was with a full sanctuary, organ playing and the reception all set and waiting. Each time I was surprised, because they had affirmed the promises they had made in my office.

They also took a vow to evaluate the marriage relationship on or near their wedding anniversary and inform me how life was going in their marriage. This was a ten year commitment, though one couple has done it for 38 years. I had found that marriages do not just come apart, but often drift apart. In any event, I had time to do what I could, to bring the marriage in out of the cold.

This was why I was blindsided by a "bride abandoned at the altar." Waiting in the bride's dressing room for over an hour, she became hysterical. My sister-in-law at the organ, was playing every wedding theme song in the book and a few I recognized she used at funerals. The sanctuary was full and folk were getting restless. The reception was ready in the social hall, but no groom. The wedding hostess was ringing her hands and the bride was sobbing. The rehearsal had gone as most do and I did not have a clue as to what I had missed. I decided we would wait ten more minutes, then the obvious had to be faced and I would make the announcement of the change in plans.

At that moment the out of breath groom and best man entered the sanctuary. First thing the groom said was, "There is no parking. We ran two blocks." Then taking a deep breath said there was a wreck on the freeway. "We were the first ones stopped."

I don't think the bride was processing all of this as she was shaking her head when I told her. Then the groom remembered the ring was still back in the car, which caused the best man to turn around and leave running to retrieve the ring. The groom was clutching the license. The bride came out of the dressing room and flew into his arms.

Now to remind you that cell phones had not been invented, that tuxedos are not gym clothes and after running as hard as they could for two blocks, you knew which way the wind was blowing without asking. After this late start, we had a joyful wedding and reception, with a rumpled groom still trying to explain, and a red-eyed bride buried deep in the arms of her beloved.

Beyond any doubt this will be an oft repeated story and surely will be requested by their children and grandchildren.

One all time classic couple wanted the services of the church and when I asked the groom if he had been married before, he answered truthfully "five times." Of course I asked what was the cause of all of these relationships ending in divorce. He said rather factually that it was alcoholism. With this clue I asked where he had met this intended. He responded quickly, "at my favorite bar…"

✳ My First Associate

It all happened because we had been appointed to serve a great congregation.

Somehow I was always blessed with gifted Ministerial Associates. It was at this church that the Pastor Parish Committee hired Ron Crandall, who was someone who stood out for good reason.

On Easter Sunday we had five services. These were alternated between the sanctuary and social hall, back to back, with Ron doing the first part five times while I followed to preach. He did this so well it was easy for me.

A love affair with a congregation

To make room for the next Easter's overflow crowd, we went to large TV sets on the lawn for the congregation, and it rained.

A word about my associate, Ron. He was on a TV show called the Dating Game. As I recall, there were four, (and he reminded me it was three) men behind a partition hidden from view. A young lady asked questions of the three she could not see and was to choose her blind date.

She chose Ron as the winner. Then the show announced that this winning couple was going on an all-expense trip to Reno. There was great applause from the audience and big excitement from both of them, followed by a quick pitch of all that they were going to experience. Then the show went to commercial.

When the cameras were turned off, she asked Ron what he did. Ron replied that he was a "Theologue". She asked what in the world was that? Ron responded that he was studying to become a minister. She just turned and walked away, meaning NO way am I going on this holiday with this strange guy.

There was a free trip to be had and Ruth's younger sister was visiting us. Bonnie had been working on TV as the weather girl. At Ruth's suggestion, Ron asked her to fill in and take the free trip. They shook hands on it. Soon a Limo took them to the airport, where they flew first class to Reno, fell in love, and the rest is history.

This is how Ron and I became family, then and now. He could not be a better brother-in-law than he is and I think he married up as did I. We added this new limb to both of our family trees. It later sprouted other limbs, which have been cause for joy as it continued its growth.

✳ A Trip with a Miracle Ending

Thursdays I had an early morning breakfast with the high school Youth Fellowship. I proposed an American Heritage tour. The trustees turned down this idea because it involved buying a bus. The verdict was no, it was, "Too much risk."

So I bought an ex-Trailways bus with borrowed money. It only had two and a half million miles on the odometer. We lined up a professional truck driver - who dropped out at the last minute. Fortunately, a friend quit his driving job to drive the bus for the tour. Ron led this summer tour across the nation with a full bus of youth looking forward to being exposed to the history of our nation. All acknowledged one thing, the onboard toilet was a disaster, but other than that it was all splendid, exciting, and a great investment.

Now the God part and why I have not spent my life

in debtor prison: On the homeward trek of the tour, somewhere in Alabama, the steering column of the bus parted. No doubt they were going at the speed limit and rolling along, putting the miles behind them. The steering wheel suddenly was free spinning, with the driver having no steering control of the bus.

At the same moment, the road made a ninety-degree banked turn to go up and over the railroad tracks. On the other side the road made a left ninety-degree banked turn, again following parallel to the railroad tracks. The driver, being the pro he was, never touched the brakes. If he had, the front wheels would have been free to turn any which way, without any restraint, and most likely would have turned sideways, overturning the bus.

Ron was leading this adventure and he did note that they ended up on the right side of the RR tracks, but on the wrong side of the highway. Because of the way this happened, I have tried to duplicate this event with my car. Taking my hands off the steering wheel at such a RR crossing, I have lost my nerve to do this every time.

Now the really scary part of all of this happened without a dime's worth of insurance. Moral, listen to the trustees. I could still be making payments on the retirements of a lot of lawyers.

Epilogue: I was backing the bus up in the church parking lot when the steering shaft broke (parted) again. I had it welded again and sold that Trailways bus for the same price I bought it. I shed no tears when I sold it, but I did do a little celebration dance and offered another thankful prayer that miracles are not out of style.

What I learned about bus shopping, while really looking for a retired Greyhound bus as my first choice. I found they had a unique wheel size, 19 inches, and the tires fit no other wheel made. This is why I went with Trailways.

This accident was always referred to by me as a God miracle, with a major number of angels assisting.

❋ Spreading the News

One job a minister had in every parish served was seldom spoken about, unless extremely well done or done poorly, yet It was expected to be done by all pastors. It was writing and editing the church newsletter. I learned this while serving our first church, and noting that the word mimeograph was spoken with stoic grim determination. Printing was always done by an overworked secretary, but is rarely appreciated. Having no secretary and never touching an A. B. Dick mimeograph, it was weeks before I got a presentable bulletin out.

Even writing for such was a new skill. I got my notice of being a failure at this back in high school. I wrote one column making fun of a whole list of teachers, which I saw as funny. That was the last thing ever accepted for ink in the "Hunter's Call" written by me.

❋ Another World

How this came about: While serving our third church, which was second in size to the downtown church, (read much smaller), I wrote a weekly editorial in our church newsletter. The very popular pastor in the downtown church wrote a weekly column for the local newspaper. He was moved to another church. I recognized the opportunity and quickly wrote three columns.

Entering the intense, chaotic, and noisy world of the local newspaper, I asked for the editor. I was pointed to a door and there he was. He was at the helm of his world, standing in his cluttered office behind his desk. Knowing I had one shot and it had to be brief, I was very brief. I laid my copy on his desk. This being on top of whatever else happened to be in his clutter. He never said a word, but did shift his cigar in a cloud of smoke as I left.

My columns appeared the next week and a note saying I was to be paid fifteen dollars a column. After two years or so he called me into my second appearance in this sacrosanct world of information for the public, by those who buy their ink by the barrel. He extended his hand and said he had suggested I be syndicated out of headquarters in Boston with Copley News Service. I wrote a weekly column for them for 28 years, and ten months.Though being fired twice, I never missed a weekly deadline. No small achievement. I never used my Copley copy in my church newspaper.

Here I can boast that I have lined more birdcages and wrapped more fish than most pastors have. Such is the small print in the life of this minister.

I later traded teaching a class on writing, having never had one, for my tuition to earn my Ph.D.

※ **Israel in View**

Fritz LeRoque had taken numerous adult work teams to Europe. He asked us why didn't we take a youth work team to help in the rebuilding still going on after WWII? Not having the slightest hope of travel, we said that sounds great. I had not used a day of my vacation time which had been saved for my family. A bombed church in Norway was contacted and they needed us, but we wound up on a kibbutz.

The Israel "Truman Tripper" story is in Part Two,

if you are interested. It all happened as we served the appointment noted here.

✳ The People Made it Happen

Things went wrong in so many ways. I had been asked to speak to the PTA by a church member who was the PTA President and this was important to her. Getting in the car, I noticed that the header boards of our new church driveway and parking lot were half an inch shy from what the contract said was what we had paid for. The crew was ready to begin putting down asphalt. It was going to be very expensive for the contractor to stop and put in three-inch headers, but I gave him no choice.

Guess what I had forgotten? The PTA president. She was embarrassed and livid, meaning she was chewing nails and spitting brads. Some days you can't win.

Next, the lady living right across the street was going to the city to stop "the ringing of those infernal bells from that new carillon." Then President Kennedy was shot and I was to speak to the student body of the local high school the next day. Of this, I have not a smidgen of memory. The whole world seemed to be in shock as was I.

At home the issue of the need for one more bedroom came to a head. One trustee, with a smile, made the motion in a trustee's meeting to put birth control pills in the budget.

A lady who walked some distance to attend church in warehouse dresses, gave me a ten thousand dollar check to start the fund for a third bedroom. Along with the check she gave us a one-dollar 1856 gold U.S. coin as a personal gift that had been in her family forever, which we still have.

The parsonage could now be remodeled and in the future, house most any family.

You guessed it. The pastor following us was a bachelor. He did a great job but said he could sleep in a different bed every night. So much for planning the future.

✳ Confirmation Skiing

To get the community to cross our church threshold, I had been buying ski stuff at garage sales. Most ski items for youth had been quickly outgrown. When I had enough, I let it be known that outgrown ski items could be donated, or parents could select replacement ski equipment which was the right size. Not a spectacular program, but it brought in a few new families.

That's when I started promising my 7th and 8th graders I would teach them how to ski, if they would stick with me through a two-year confirmation program. They hung in there like glue for the two-year program and I got to go skiing.

We had a new city program called Head Start and we began by filling up our new education building five days a week. This was for low-income families and our family qualified. In addition we had a thriving nursery school working out of the same building.

Meanwhile, while remodeling the parsonage, I was painting a door as the finishing touch of a new bath and bedroom. The phone rang. It was the District Superintendent asking us to consider taking another appointment. NO! was our response. We had only been here five years. He asked us to just take a look at this possible appointment, so we checked it out. We came back with a firm absolute, "NO, but thanks anyway."

Two weeks later, we were told the D.S. had a heart attack and all appointments in pencil were now set in concrete. So we were moved, dragging our feet to a new world of social unrest, strangers, and a parsonage that needed help.

My last act at the church we were leaving was to place three stainless steel crosses on the outside wall of our new classroom and auditorium in memory of the three boy scouts who drowned on an outing. They were not from our troop, but their parents were in the membership.

One burr under the pulpit robe was a wonderful friend who sat in the choir right behind me. During any sermon, he would quietly say things such as "Do you really believe that?" or something funny to throw me off track, but other than that bit of fun at my expense, he was a great and wonderful friend.

At our last service at this beloved church, every pew was packed. It was hard leaving this church because most of the congregation was our age, and like every church we had served, we loved them and they loved us.

X

APPOINTMENT #4

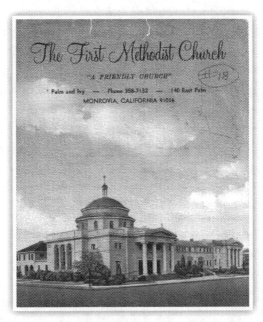

Unique building and time to let ministry happen

❋ Half a City Block

Our new place of service where we were appointed was waiting for us in downtown Monrovia. The L.A. Times had just referred to this suburb as boring.

The church was built in 1912, with incredibly thick walls and no steel reinforcing, but this old edifice had withstood the shaking ground of numerous earthquakes. The sanctuary still had an ice chute where air was blown over the ice, and thus they had modest air conditioning. Of course they also had a coal chute for making steam heat. This had long ago gone out of use.

In the library there hung every pastor's picture since the last century, which seemed to me before time began. Looking at these long gone ministers with their photo eyes following me, I always felt I was under their judgement. Many of the former pastors before the 1940's had long beards and I didn't. "Hanging the pastor" was a tradition I guess is still being observed.

The unique thing about the building was that it had appeared in a number of movies, mostly as a courthouse complex that took in half a city block. Memory says there were a great number of pianos, mostly in the three story Sunday school building.

This was sure going to be a challenge, and maybe an opportunity, if I lasted that long.

❋ Drugs Bigtime

We knew we had been living in a Norman Rockwell world. It was our fifth year, and things could not have been going any better. It was so good that you would have needed a prescription to buy this level of joy.

Now, if I were any greener, knowing about the world of drugs, the cows would have eaten me. You get the picture. It was wonderful and tough to leave all we had accomplished.

Our new community could not have been more

different, as drugs were everywhere. There could not have been a bigger contrast between the appointments.

But we had been transferred to a new, to us, church, and being out of my depth was an understatement. I was introduced to the church secretary. She had been there before me, and she told me that she would be there when I was gone. Translated, she was the church secretary, not mine. So Ruth and I tightened our belts and hired out of our pocket, a wonderful competent secretary. The church soon put her in the church budget.

Speaking of budget, something I was asked to do far more than I ever expected to do, were the many funerals that I was called on to conduct. This may have been because of a mortuary being next door to the church. We could now marry or bury on short notice.

Now that I was there, what was I to do? The problem at hand was that the young people were going up to the drug center of Haight-Ashbury, the Mecca of the pot/drug cult. Having an unused parsonage next to the church, we opened a drop-in, stay awhile, center. I asked the city for money for staff and expenses, and got it.

I really think the townspeople didn't know what to do about the kids and drugs, and because the church was doing something, I became the Crime Commissioner on the City Council. This opened the door to the Rotary Service Club to fill the one slot for clergy. The part that still causes me to smile is when my picture was taken with the Mayor. He always stood on a block of wood to even our height. I am 5' 14".

In addition, we had a massive, three quarters of a city block, unused basement. We created an 1880 ice cream parlor with piano, pool tables, ping pong, and air shuffleboard for an after school place to drop-in. The spot was a great idea, except for the three mistakes I made, because this was all new to me.

The first error was inviting the art class at the local high school to do creative art painting on the walls. Remember, this was the sixties. My second misjudgment was that I failed to mention that the theme was an old-time ice-cream parlor, meaning horse and buggy, hoop skirts, and anything else from the 1890's. What they painted were pictures of the music group, The Grateful Dead. This was done in paint that responded to ultraviolet light -- so with UV flashing light, we could give aspirin a headache.

This led to the big one. Noting that it would be smart to have a host for this after school drop-in center, I hired a young couple who seemed to me to be all American, reminding me of my youth radio program, "Jack Armstrong, The All American Boy". This was a hand-in-glove fit until I found they were selling drugs. He disappeared. She confessed she was hooked on drugs. I took her to the Camarillo Mental Health Center. During the registration, she must have climbed out of a bathroom window and disappeared. I never saw her again.

The saving element was the gifted, talented associate, Bruce, who knew what the chatter was among the kids and the music they were listening to. Soon we proposed a post-football game dance, with a name band. Bruce knew the unknown start-up bands and he hired them. We tried it, the word got out, and soon it was a full house. We had a winner.

So now we had wildly painted walls, and every Friday night a rock and roll band would show up, and the kids would migrate to the church basement. I sat cross-legged on a 6x8' Persian rug in the corner, and got an education talking with anyone who wanted to talk in confidence.

Church adults did the patrolling and it all worked and life was good again.

Our biggest attendance was nine hundred and ninety-four with a then unknown band called Led Zeppelin. The Association was the next big draw. I am not sure if I would have hired them to mow my lawn, but the kids loved them.

※ Unexpected Joy

We had a joyful time doing the unthinkable. One such item was taking out half of the pews to put on a play which was our Easter Cantata, "My Heart Is Glad", with an orchestra. It played to a full house.

Another unthinkable item was paying ten thousand dollars to have the church painted, which was badly needed. We did not have any hope for that kind of extra cash, so we decided to do it ourselves on Saturdays. It only took a year and three months, but it was well worth it. The adage among pastors is that in a work bee, the pastor gets stung, but here, not so.

Two asides: I asked for a volunteer to assist me to paint the cupola on top of the dome of the church. A trumpet player in "Les Brown's Band Of Renown" said he would help me. Secured by ropes we got this done while hanging on with one hand and painting with the other.

The second item occurred after all the volunteer workers had left and I was alone in the dark, sitting on the curb in my grungy work clothes, cleaning paint rollers and brushes. I admit I dried the rollers on the street. A couple stopped in a car and asked who I was. Of course, I answered that I was the Sr. Pastor, despite the paint spatter. I will never forget their response because it can be taken two ways. "Sure you are!."

Then they called the Police. The Police soon realized they knew me, so I went home a free man and not to be a guest at the Gray Bar Hotel. Working closely with the Police Chief as a City Councilman, I found he pretended to be tough as nails, with his ever-present cigar, but underneath he was a pussy cat with the hobby of photographing hummingbirds.

The humor in this was that the police never used the front door to the police station. They parked in the back of the station and used the back door. I, being new, used the front entrance. My guess is that sometime in the past, someone emptied their pockets of seeds because there was a rather large bush of marijuana growing beside the front door. I was somewhat cautious bringing up that as an issue that had best be tended to ASAP.

We had fun with the congregation. The organ sat in a recess (hole) beside the pulpit. One Sunday morning Ruth sat in that hole with the organist. She had in her hand a microphone. I preached and in my remarks, I made a positive statement of faith. Ruth cut into the sound system with, "You don't really believe that do you?" or "That's silly!" The ushers were on their feet running, looking for who this was that had cut into our sound system. Ruth and I had a discussion on faith and the full attention of the congregation. We apologized to the ushers.

✳ Free as a Bird

During the year I figured out how to approximate a birdlike experience of freedom in the air, close as it was, but really nothing like it. I started scattering human ashes at sea provided by my mortician friends. At our local airport, there were several small planes for rent. One had a hopper on the wingtip but the rental price was infected with price gouging.

The problem was that the wind currents around a flying aircraft would, with malice, blow all the ashes back into the cockpit. I figured a way to beat this, and it worked. I had several pilots ask me how this was done, but I never passed on such. I protected my slice of the business world and got my flight time paid for.

First, pre-flight the plane, most often a Cessna 150. Next, run up the engine and check each of the magnetos, release the brakes and then shake, rattle and roll. Then I moved in a cloud of dust, smoke, and noise. The plane lifted from the earth like a sick angel, but left nonetheless, the tenacious ever present grip of gravity.

Navigation was VFR (Visual Flight Rules). What led me to the beach was a wide brown highway of dead lawns. It was where the state was going to build the Santa Monica Freeway. I had to be three miles out over the ocean and then I throttled back. Having figured that there were strong air currents under the plane from airspeed and prop wash turbulence, I put the craft just next to the edge of a stall, opened the cabin door, made the plane start a slow left turn, reached down with a paper bag full of ashes, and with a finger tore the sack as near the underside as I could reach. Success! Clean cabin. The prop wash took the ashes under the plane and now I could get some flight time and be paid for doing so. By law I could only scatter one set of ashes at a time and had to touch down back at Santa Monica each time.

When I did this at Christmas time, I found myself looking forward to seeing all the lights; however I only caught glimpses of Yule decoration as they are, for the most part, on the front or eaves of homes. On the fourth of July, I also tried seeing firework displays, but only saw clouds of smoke which brightened up every few moments under the smoke.

In any event, I had a lot of mini-vacations poking holes in the sky with the exception of near misses with other aircraft in the dark, the fog or smog, on approach back to mother earth.

✳ Preach or Write?

While serving this parish I had to become serious about the column I was writing for the local paper. Because I was syndicated, it cost editors, in ads, to pick up my column.

About the tenth year, I was fired. This was done by phone from Boston. I called back and asked if I could meet the editor face to face as a learning experience. I was told to go to the San Diego Union & Tribune, the West coast Copley paper that carried my column.

This meant I could get one and maybe two columns in before the ax spoke the last word. I ended each column by offering the reader something free, such as ten rules about something. It was theirs by sending a stamped envelope letter to the San Diego paper.

It worked. I had a full mailbag waiting for me when I appeared at the editor's door. They never mentioned my being fired.

I am still giving thanks and recognition to a lady saint, who earned multiple hallelujahs, who for fourteen years corrected my copy and answered my column mail, and for nine years housed a 1926 Studebaker in her garage that I was restoring.

Later, at the San Diego news office, with my column in hand, an employee said he wanted to show me something. He took my writing and put it in a machine that sent it in minutes to Boston. He handed it back to me saying it is now set in type as it was received, and will be printed when called for, and be on the street in minutes. I was impressed by what is now "old hat."

※ A Midnight Desert Wedding

One wedding I had made the newspapers, with reporters attending. The guests were one verb away from throwing a punch, but an agreed truce held. No guests sat down as there were no chairs. It was held at midnight in the Mojave Desert with no moon, many cameras, no fighting, no drugs and no directions where it was to be held except by some herd instinct. Decorations were cactus and tumbleweeds.

The couple wanting to tie the knot, were beyond doubt committed to sealing their lives into one and to do it with God's blessing. I have no memories of any counseling I had with them. They were different, but very much in love, and they wanted the benefit of clergy. What set them apart was that they were members of two different off-road (dirt bike) motorcycle clubs. Both clubs were committed to "Hare and Hound" desert racing and were very competitive.

If you have never heard of this, you have chosen your friends with wisdom. Riding dirt bikes with horse power more in the number associated with semi-trucks, they rode rickoshaying off of rocks, and were airborne a lot. They are certified mad, in my observation.

The groom appeared normal and was not a knuckle dragger but was a competitive rider and seemed normal. The bride was attractive, well spoken and was a mechanic of the other bike club. Why I was chosen to perform this knot tying was I was the chaplain of the Clean Sweep team to which neither of them belonged, thus neutral. I had been given a Clean Sweep jacket but I sure didn't wear it that night.

My bit in all of this was I got seriously lost trying to find them, because the place they had chosen for the wedding was great for bikes, but I was driving a French Renault Dolphin. Hoping someone had a CB radio, I got on top of a hill, got their signal, and found my way.

It was a wedding by the book, but no hands were counted when I asked if anyone objected to why this couple should not be united in marriage, but I believe that every hand was in the air.

Love transcends motorcycle gangs

The story appeared in the newspapers with multiple pictures. I was a bike rider myself, riding a Honda 450 rice burner, which served me quite well. But it was after too many rider's funerals that I found myself refering to them as "murder cycles." This came home to me when I saw our sixteen year old son doing a wheelie on my Honda. That was the day I sold it.

I had been appointed to serve under the newly elected governor, George Deukmejian, on the Motorcycle Safety committee. My suggestion for a safety campaign was

"Heads without helmets go splat." It was not accepted, but I thought this said all that needed to be said. Now back to the wedding.

I found the site or they found me. The two clubs were standing apart shaking their heads, no doubt about this preacher that had been lost. We had a wedding, even if the couple wore different logos on their leathers. They said their vows and the stars above brightened a bit in their watchful twinkling.

After the vows were said, her club congratulated her, then his club. But any club loyalty that existed broke down as they mingled, talked, kidded each other and shared memories. Later the couple and I became great friends and they kept their vows till "death did them part." Now they are together in the place that the Creator of all has gone ahead to prepare for us as He promised.

The question back at the church was "Your minister did WHAT?"

✻ Kids Will Be Kids

We started two nursery schools, the profit from one paying for the other so it could be below cost for those who could not afford the morning school. This was tightly held information about scholarships offered, when needed.

We also added a counseling center. It was the Boy Scout troop that gave me the most satisfaction until I found that the Scout Master had been a fighter pilot in the German Luftwaffe in WWII. This I was not prepared for, but he was a good Scoutmaster and I didn't ask any more questions and they did salute the American flag.

Our personal problem was our sons. Ruth sang in the choir so they were left to sit alone. One Sunday morning worship service I saw members of the congregation looking startled. It turned out that it was our youngest crawling on the floor under the pews, through the congregation. Later I observed them and other kids in the balcony shooting spit wads at the hats below.

The unsolved mystery was who had written in a hymnal in the balcony "under the bed" after every hymn title.

Come to think of it, one older son had a good start burning down the parsonage. He had a good fire going out behind the garage before we smelled the smoke. We had a lively time at dinner as these items were brought up.

I was reminded of a story told by a fellow Methodist minister who had been a Revivalist Evangelist in the deep South. He preached and his wife sang and their son who was five, was cutting up in the front row. Dad's signals to knock it off were ignored. Sermon over, dad came down and picked up his errant son, putting him over his shoulder, and marched his wayward boy to the exit. The boy, knowing what was coming, said to the congregation, "YOU ALL PRAY FOR ME, YOU HEAR?"

Our own children needed prayer also.

XI

HERE WE GO AGAIN

Building a brand new church

❋ A Special Place

Things became wonderfully normal where we were. Our oldest son graduated from high school, the middle son played his first drum solo, and our daughter was learning to sculpt in mash potatoes at the dining room table and in clay at school.

One of our cats was stealing socks out of the neighbor's laundry. Our youngest son would not go into the public plunge with the excuse, "Too many Scottish people in that pool," meaning African Americans. Our nearsighted cat would chase a bird off a cement fence and take a blind nose dive as it stepped off the end of the wall. All was normal until . . .

It was our daughter who set up our next move. She had gone with her class to the Renaissance Fair in Agoura Hills, and came back home asking "Oh Daddy, can we ever be appointed to a place like that?" I explained that there was only a very small rural church there with a handful of people. It couldn't happen. Two weeks later a District Superintendent called and asked if we would like to start a church.

Seems the D.S, Dr. Richard Cain, had bought prime ground which was to become the most prominent corner of a place yet to be, all for the price of a dollar a square foot. This was too exciting to pass up, so we moved.

As we were packing, a desperate call came from a mortician friend to do a last-minute service. This left Ruth and the kids to finish the packing. They packed everything, and unknowingly included the ashes of several persons which I had not yet air scattered. Later Ruth asked me what these copper boxes held... I am not sure she has forgiven me yet, having moved three bodies with our stuff.

Moving had a big problem. There was no parsonage to move to. So we and a van of our belongings moved in with my folks in their two-bedroom house. This was in Van Nuys and I commuted to what was called Westlake Village. It took a while to find a place where we could hang our hat, and get financing to purchase a house that was to be the church parsonage and our future home.

The octagonal real estate office for the area was to be replaced and had been given to the Methodist church to be moved to the new property. We asked the Lutheran congregation to join us, led by a living saint, Rev. Bob Lawson, who was a brother in our faith and a gifted Pastor. Temple Adat Elohim was forming and needed a place to hold services, so they were invited to hold their services on Saturday. It was dubbed Covenant House.

During an earthquake, an out of breath man entered the sanctuary and told me this had to be the safest place in town. During the Christmas season the Christmas tree was placed in a wagon. Our Hebrew friends called it a Hanukkah Bush.

✳ Growing Pains

Having three services on a Sunday morning called for critical timing. I held a Methodist service at 9:00 a.m. The Lutheran service started at 10:00, and another Methodist service at 11:15, so my recurring nightmare was, the Lutherans were waiting at the front door looking at their watches. "The Lutherans are coming! The Lutherans are coming!"

In preparation for converting the gift of a real estate office into a church, a large dish of adobe was removed where the building was to sit. This was replaced with sand so all air ducts were under the church.

Great idea except when it rained, the adobe held the water and the air ducts flooded, resulting in a rainstorm in the church. For the nine years we were appointed there, I had to pump the rainwater out of the ducts or else sell out to the Baptists. So the wife's phrase was, "Get out of bed, it's raining!" which always sent me to the church, with the pump in hand.

New folk moving into the community made all of this a downhill pull as we went from being what Lyle Shaller called our church a "Lap " church to manage, to being almost a ranch church. That is, until the gasoline crisis ended and all the jobs that had been frozen were now up for moving. This is when I found that IBM stood for "I've Been Moved."

That year the church lost every office holder and what really hurt, every Sunday School teacher. It was like starting over and our kids discovered they weren't the only ones who were moved because of their dad's job.

What happened to me at a Christmas Eve service was a bit of a shock, never to ever be repeated. A visitor/parent handed me a key. He then quietly gave me a pink slip and said that the bus "was outside." That bus was a shot in the arm for our youth program. The giver thought I owned the church so all bus items were made out in my name. The Trustees took care of that and the "Brown Hound" joined our staff. A brand new church from the ground up needs everything. We now had a bus.

I truly believe the events of my life are in the love of my Creator's Will for my life unless... It was providential that in conversation I had after a funeral, when the widow asked me if I knew what she could do with her late husband's organ? He had taught organ at Pasadena City College. Our new church now had an organ at the right price, so we had it rebuilt to ensure long and faithful service.

Making the most of our windfall, and making the most of the dedication, I asked Gaylord Carter, organist at Dodger Stadium, to play the dedication service. Gaylord, during this service, demonstrated what playing classical J. Bach on the organ was like. He asked for the name of a hymn and he began to play it with one hand while calling out for another hymn. I called out " Battle Hymn Of The Republic" which he began to play with his feet. Then someone called for their favorite hymn and he played all three at the same time.

Then he stopped and announced, "Now you know what it is like to play Bach on the organ." Of course, at a later point in the concert, the organ gasped, groaned and gave up and quit. Gaylord just moved to the piano and finished the concert. A church member took the organ home and rebuilt it again for his personal use, and recently checking, I found that it is still giving good service, but the owner said he has never attempted playing Bach.

✳ A New Way to Heaven

It was a gift to me from myself.

We saved our vacation days all year, though knee walking tired at Christmas and sick after Lent and Easter. All vacation days were taken by us at once for serious family trips or mountain camping. On one of the last vacation days, I had the family wait as I took for myself a special time, joining with the angels by soaring in a rented glider. I, for a moment of time, "slipped the surly bonds of earth and…" rode the currents of the sky and clouds. It was as close to what I thought being intoxicated must be like without the headache or the porcelain throne embrace.

I was towed by a plane to about 2,000 feet, then I pulled the red knob and released the tow rope. It was suddenly absolutely quiet. After a moment I could only hear the bubbles of air flowing over the canopy. Rolling over to a line of hills to catch the updraft and gain a bit of altitude, I soon found a strong quiet thermal elevator up. I rode this current of air climbing, smiling and circling.

An eagle was riding the same current of up air as I was. This majestic bird was only moving the very minuscule end tips of its wings and making three circles in the thermal to my one. It was only after it sailed off that I remembered I had my Nikon camera hung around my neck and had not taken a picture of what was so close and a once in my lifetime opportunity.

My other well-remembered event while treading where angels dwell: I was in the pattern of making a landing in a sailplane. Making my approach for a landing, I was taking my half out of the middle and doing so without thought or guilt.

Gliders have the right of way, since they have only a stick, rudder, and the seat of the pants of the pilot for control. Being much slower in the landing pattern, a prop plane joined in the pattern behind me. He was making tight S's to keep his airspeed up. He was telling me he was impatient, which I ignored. I took all the time possible to make this powered aircraft pilot wait his turn to put his wheels on the tarmac. I smugly stretched my landing. This turned into shock when I saw his prop stop and knew he was out of fuel. I dropped as fast as I could and quickly turned off of the runway onto the grass beside it. I then escaped, not ever wanting to meet him face to face, ever.

Doing this was the crescendo of our vacation before facing all that was waiting for me on my church office desk.

❊ Christmas in a Wagon

It was crazy, but I knew Rev. Richard Brooks who made what was crazy, work. We would meet early on Saturday morning, and have breakfast. I would listen, ask questions, and get to work. As Rev. Brooks had his congregation building a big beautiful sanctuary, I learned how to have my congregation build a social hall for three congregations.

An option before the church was to trade our prime land for a turn-key sanctuary and social hall built elsewhere. We said no. They added a nursery school. It was still no deal. The congregation built that too.

Pete Candreva was our member architect but I soon learned that not everyone can read blueprints. Every Saturday was a workday for us while the Temple Adat Elohim held services in the sanctuary. Helping to keep the peace was Rabbi Richard Address. He and I did a weekly radio show and we both really enjoyed doing this honest and free conversation.

✳ Making Room for People

What I never even hoped for was a volunteer who knew how and where to get things donated or below wholesale. He saved us gobs of money.

The bid was 10 thousand dollars to tile the roof of our much needed social hall. I hired a tile man to teach me how to install the clay tile roof needed to finish. Then I taught those who volunteered how to do the laying of the tile roofing. It was labor-intensive but worth it. The final counting noted that the new social hall cost an unheard of $28.14 per square foot.

I went to one of the older California Missions (San Luis Obispo, 1772), and asked for and received an old clay roofing tile that was used as a cap tile. On the underside, I had the children who came forward for the children's story, sign the tile. If memory serves me correctly, there were 65 children from the two services who made their mark. Bill Locklear, the director of housing at UCLA, and I, set that last tile in place.

Taking no credit, our newly hired youth minister, Al

Ludington, set up Sunday School classes to be eight weeks long and take place between the services. Teachers were asked to present what they would teach. The kids would then choose what class they would take.

Most popular was writing the script of a story Jesus told, then videotaping what they acted out. The second most popular class was 4th century B.C. jewelry making. Then came turning wool into cloth, etc. For this, it is best to have someone who knows the subject, which we did. And we had a filled Sunday School and unhappy parents who wanted to go visit grandparents.

❉ Sleep Interruption

It was always in the early a.m. that she called. The calls happened more and more often and when she did, I knew she was off of her meds. While it cost me some sleep, it was part of my life as a Pastor. The wake up call could be a call for help, so the phone was always answered.

Then the calls were suddenly different. It wasn't her. I didn't recognize the voices of those who rang us early in the wee hours of the morning and the callers weren't asking for help. I listened and figured these persons could have had too much adult beverage, often having marriage problems or had a theological question settled in early church history, or a sports team action I knew nothing about, but background voices were there also.

Ruth is blessed with the gift of sound sleep, but I would ask the caller to wait a moment as I put on a robe and went downstairs to the other phone. This happened often enough, I started to pay attention. Different callers all calling from the same number?

In time I found that someone had written something

about me on an unknown barroom men's bathroom wall with my home phone number. I finally asked a kind voice of such a caller to scratch out my phone number. Now it was back to, "did you take your meds?"

✳ Field to Sky

First a reminder that it was the 1970's and brides were trying to outdo each other in the bazaar places they chose to say their nuptial vows. Yes, I had my chance to perform weddings in strange and improbable places. So how did I wind up in a knee high weed field having a couple pledge and say their vows making them one?

The groom's dad was the pro-bono architect on our social hall and nursery school. His son was a carpenter who trusted a temporary banister on the second floor and ended up in the hospital. When he recovered he asked me to do his wedding. I could not say anything but yes.

Turning a weed lot into a wedding chapel

This was to be a "A Hot Air Balloon wedding." The invitation said "Casual Dress." All guests were to gather in a doughnut shop at sunrise in some unremembered town. We were a bit early or they were late, but the shock was that the bride and bridesmaids were dressed in beautiful gowns; the men were in tuxedos, while Ruth and I wore casual clothes. We had donuts and coffee, met all of the guests and friends, and as the sun showed its face, we moved on to a field with knee high weeds.

The balloons were all carried on or in trailers. The balloons were blobs of confusion until spread out on the ground. Then they were propped open mouthed, and large butane burners were lit off with a roar. There were seven balloons, so multiply the noise by seven. It was noticeable as the balloons took shape, just how big they were and no two were alike.

It was then that I realized that the dresses of the women in the wedding party were the same colors as their balloons. This was a laughing, fun loving crowd. My old fogy self relaxed as the weeds were tramped down. Yes, I had concerns for the bride's dress being dragged through the weeds, but more so for the fire danger. They all knew what they were doing and were having a good time doing it.

Soon all of the balloons were united with their baskets and made an umbrella roof. This formed a covering over the wedding party, in this wedding-in-the-field chapel. All became silent which was my clue to begin. The service went well and when I introduced them as husband and wife all seven fired up their balloons with a roar to celebrate with the newly wedded couple.

Then we guests climbed into the waiting baskets and went up and up and away. There was no wind so 'away' is overstating what was taking place. As we watched the rising balloon below us come up directly beneath the basket next to us, it tilted their basket, looking as if it was going to dump its load of wedding guests. At the last moment it moved slightly, sliding past, and avoiding a disastrous ending to an exciting wedding.

✳ Climbing the Mountain

There are things we all do that are nothing, but later mean a lot. I asked our son Tim if he wanted to climb Mt. Whitney with me. He must have said yes because we did. He was fourteen or so, and was handicapped with a bad back. One set of doctors suggested he have a steel rod implanted, and others suggested a body cast, all a tough row of corn to hoe for a high school student.

This outing was no small thing for him to undertake. We didn't shorten the handle of our toothbrush to save weight, but no tent was considered. My backpack was fully loaded and I packed his back pack as light as I dared, so he had a real part in this assault up the tallest mountain in the lower '48.

If you turn west at Lone Pine, the road leads to Whitney Portals. Lots of talk between us, passing through one of California's awesome scenic drives. Out of the car, hoist on the back pack and hit the trail. Little conversation, just keep moving. Rest now and then, get up and plod on up the trail.

Stop and look at a lake, and decide to make camp. Gather wood, cook dinner, pick the pine needles out of the coffee and not mention what we both in our haste forgot. Dark drew its curtain. Roll out our bedrolls in the shelter of a downed Pine serving as a windbreak, and talk about the day.

The stars lit up the heavens. What I was not prepared for were the rats Investigating us, at least I hoped that was what they were. Tim asked, and what could I say? I used the parent thing about him needing his sleep.

The sun soon made itself known, and hunger got us to fix breakfast. We left our backpacks there and hiked up the rest of the 14,505 feet to the top.

This you have to see for yourself. With a spur of looking ahead, I picked up a rock. I gave it to Tim on his 21st birthday to never forget this moment between us.

✻ Uh Oh...

Serving this congregation for nine years we were ready to have the congregation vote on the plans for a new sanctuary. It seemed things could not go better. The congregation had grown from the few visionary founders to around 800 plus, and was full of commited, enthusiastic people. I was having a blast.

Out calling on a family who I noted was missing church more often than not. They had given the church the Brown Hound. My innermost motive was to see if they might underwrite the cost of a steeple holding a carillon.

While in this family's front room selling this investment, the phone rang and it was Jean, the all-doing church secretary, informing me I was wanted at Methodist Headquarters, ASAP. The Bishop and his cabinet were waiting.

There I was informed we were to move, and where was yet to be decided.

I had turned down the Bishop to take the editorship of the Conference Newspaper, "Circuit Rider," which Bishop Golden had offered me. He found this an unusual response, a non pleaser as he was not used to being told "NO!" I also turned down this offer of a move.

After some intense negotiating, the Bishop brought it all to a conclusion with the words, "Either move or turn in your papers." I folded, and after a talk with Ruth, we did as we were told. That's how close Westlake came to maybe having a highly visible steeple, or tower with bells announcing the hours and sundown vespers.

This time we went to our new appointment with me dragging both of my feet. I admit I was depressed and angry. I had kept my withdrawal card from the Operating Engineers Union and considered reinstating it.

This was the all-time low point. Still, I could not walk away from the ministry.

Just a personal note: During those nine years three of our children graduated from Agoura High School, our oldest started college, then switched to radio school, and both Ruth and I earned a Ph.D. We were now a "real paradox." But that's another story.

XII

INTO THE INNER CITY

Accept it or turn in your papers

✳ A Friend in Deed

It was a painful parting after nine years serving this parish, with all of the stories that made it more than we could ever put on this word canvas. The downside shock of being told to uproot and move or turn in my ordination papers, was painfully hard. Our faith has a message that we believe and know to be trustworthy and proven to be true. Our lives can be guided beyond any understanding on our part. We all bring the life problems we have with us, as we live out our days.

This world had a steep learning curve. After I made my peace with my Lord and forgave the Bishop, a priceless gift came my way. The saving grace was an incredible friend, working for what he called being a "spook" in a think tank in DC. He took two days off, and flew to California. His purpose was to turn me around by believing this could be God's plan for us.

He was what I needed. The kind of guy and God's person to lift my chin off the ground and be told to either move to an unknown church or end my being a pastor. Forever grateful, Harry Foulkrod. Thank you beyond any words I have.

Hidden in his words of faith was the simple message, if I had a lemon, make lemonade.

❋ Rest...Then Obey

We found a whole different kind of church. It was a downtown, high steeple, and truly beautiful cathedral. It was also a modestly filled sanctuary on Sunday morning, but no children, which I learned the hard way.

Our former appointment presented us with a two week holiday in Hawaii, which was no small thank you gift. On the beach, we were approached by a lad who had his arms covered selling seashell necklaces. I asked him how much for all of them? I am sure he had never been asked that question before, but we struck a deal for all he had. I was now prepared for my first Sunday Children's Sermon, wondering if I had enough for our children's time at our new assignment.

The time came in the first Sunday service in our new

appointment for all of the children to come forward. A mother pushed her reticent son out into the central aisle and he, with his head down, shuffled up to where I was. He was the only youngster in church. We both were red-faced embarrassed.

That week there was a potluck dinner to welcome us. Being used to time being flexible for arrival, Ruth and I were right on time and found the church dining hall basement filled and quiet, all waiting for me to pray grace. We learned this was and had to be a different kind of ministry than anything we had known.

❋ City Power

Nosing around, I found that the power center of the town was in the Lion's Service Club, so I put Rotary on hold and joined the Lions.

The goal was to open a nursery school. State regulations said there had to be seventy-five square feet of space per child. At the church grounds, there was enough for less than one child. Here is the "God" act in my faith world.

The city council voted that we could count the city park across the street for the space we needed. This was possible because I had my feet under the luncheon table at different times with the mayor, police chief, or city councilmen. With this major breakthrough, we opened a second baby care center for single mothers who worked. We had their trust to care for their bundle from heaven.

The fine print somewhere said we had to have one caregiver for every four babies. Financing this was not possible, so the second cause of rejoicing was that the city picked up the cost.

Now we had young adults in service, and I had chapel

service in the nursery school which was simple stories, singing, and a lot of fun for them and me. I am not sure I could do this today, but those who wanted a hug, lined up and they got a hug, a word and a kiss on the head.

Something had to be done about the gloomy sanctuary. The chandeliers were ornate but let little light down to read by. Every bid was dollars with lots of zeros, so we bought a number of used shower doors, and found a glass cutter. When these were installed in the chandeliers, we had light that brightened the whole sanctuary. The congregation could see the bulletin and read the words to the hymns. Smiles abounded.

✳ A Baptism to Remember

There are unnumbered responsibilities in the office of being a pastor, but at the top of my list was the joy of infant baptism. I always knew beyond the shadow of any doubt that a miracle was taking place. The baby that I held in my arms was also an awesome miracle. I always expected a miracle.

I had to celebrate and confirm all of this, by holding the baby fresh from God, for the sacrament of baptism. I baptized the baby while on my knees. Here was God's promise kept, as we in our denomination believe. No act on our part earned what this meant and stood for. It is God's freely given Grace.

I know what I have just written is a subject which opens many different views on the sacrament of Holy Baptism. They are all valued and honestly respected.

I wrote a letter to each baby, telling what had happened and what it meant. It was addressed to the child to be opened in ten years, and sealed with sealing wax imprinted with a cross. This was done mostly to keep nosey grandparents from opening it and reading what I had written. It ended by advising the child to go talk to their pastor and ask any questions they might have about what had taken place and its meaning.

As I voiced the words of our denomination's ritual for infant baptism, I had the God chosen co-creators (parents) put their hands on me and the other members of the family put their hands on the parents.

Here I always had my mike turned on. It had a switch to turn it off because I sang the hymns of our faith "lustily", meaning I didn't need amplification. I didn't have a solo voice, nor always stay on tune, as it was nicely put by those who asked for such a turn off switch for my mike.

After the baptism, I took pure pleasure as I went forth showing off the newly baptized child, carrying him or her down the center aisle while the whole congregation sang the song, "He's Got the Whole World In His Hand," then "This Baby in His Hands," then the baby's name, etc.

On one particular baptism, I had forgotten to turn off my mike and was singing joyfully as baby and I paraded down the center aisle. The baby stared at me, then put his hands over both ears, and the congregation almost rolled on the floor laughing.

❈ Weddings to Spare

An unorthodox form of evangelism came to mind. Having a classical sanctuary that lent itself to weddings, we made candelabras that fit on the end of the pews, with lots of candles in the altar area. Taking out ads in wedding magazines, I was in the wedding business. I set up an eight-week revolving course and time with each couple, establishing a personal relationship as their pastor. A very few joined the church, but when the baby came into the picture, we had a naming/thanksgiving/baptism service, and a nursery school waiting.

An old saying I heard somewhere: "Horses sweat, men perspire, and women glow." In one big afternoon wedding, with the bride highly adorned amidst all of the candles, she was "glowing," big time. I resolved in the middle of all of their vows somehow to get air conditioning. It had been looked into and rejected long before. I found all the necessary items had been stubbed out when the building was built, but forgotten.

Two problems prevailed. First, the noise of the compressors large enough to do the job carried throughout the building, and second, the start-up power was way beyond the load the wiring could carry. Balancing the AC compressors on an existing partition cement block wall, with them sitting crossways, answered that problem. Having a number of smaller compressors with staggered starts, solved a twenty-five-year-old problem.

No preacher can have favorites among those he/she serves, but I had one lady, Mrs. Ames, whom I held special. She was a Civil War widow. Obviously, she had married very young with this explanation, "I chose to be an old man's darling rather than a young man's slave." She had no interest in her husband's papers or diary. She gave me such and I found that he had been a Union soldier who had been wounded in the Battle Of The Wilderness, a horrific time of the late great conflict between the states.

I modeled an eight-inch statue of private Mr. Ames, standing with one leg on a rock with all of his Union gear on. I know I was showing off, but I first took this statue to the office before taking it to give to Mrs. Ames. I was told she had died that morning.

✳ Meeting the Martyrs

Looking back over the years and recalling the churches I had pastored, there were many souls that had been entrusted to our care. Beyond any question, we were blessed with gifted, dedicated lay people on every memory page. All were special in different ways, even as we are unique beings as ministers.

Among all of the special talented leaders in worship are those who also led us with the gift of music, singing and at both piano and organ. Each musician was unique. All were special, and they all enriched the service with their special gift of praying with their hands and sometimes their feet. Without question, all offered a very special gift to those of us who entered the sanctuary to worship.

Remember the organist who worked in a bar, got off at 2 a.m. then drove up the mountain and slept in his car until it was time for church? Years later he visited us and invited me to attend an Episcopal monastery in Santa Barbara for a week of soul renewal. I truly needed time out, so without a thought I said, "Sure, let's go."

It was a deep life renewal for me. A very personable monk welcomed us at the door. We were seated and he outlined what the procedure would be. It sounded like just what I needed. The big rule was no speaking from that moment, which was a bend in the road I had not anticipated.

This gracious monk was likable in an instant. We chatted and he smiled a lot. Then he told us how our time there was going to be. He said it was going to be very quiet; no talking for any reason. Translated, if you needed a bit of salt at dinner, you did not ask for the salt to be passed. You did without. A monk, not being aware of your needs, stood by.

Another Monk during dinner time stood in something like a pulpit, breaking the silence as he read the lives of those who had been martyred. It affected me so deeply that later, seeing an oil painting of one of those whom he read about in a shop in Damascus, Jordan, I did some world-class haggling and bought it. I hung it in my office and it was so misunderstood, I eventually removed it.

But I did tell my incoming confirmation students the story of a Roman Centurion who became a believer in Jesus as God and how Emperor Nero ordered his command to kill him because only Nero was god. No one in the command would give him a fatal wound.

This monastery break gave me time to slow down and pray, think, examine my values, and be renewed. The silence was loud at first but turning off the noise was wonderful. It was a rich and rewarding experience that I covet for all who want a deeper faith ground on which to build their life. I did not know that I needed this soul repair. Sad to say, this Holy retreat center, a beautiful, restful place of spiritual renewal to cure soul rot, years later was caught in a firestorm and is no more.

❋ A Busy Place

Here are a couple of things that invited the non-churched to cross the church threshold. We had an incredible organ and an organist to make it say so. Being one block from downtown and across the street from a city park, we had noon organ concerts. They were free, with an invitation to eat your lunch in the sanctuary to good music. The only complaint came from the janitor. A sixth grade teacher brought her class and certainly this was a high point for me.

Better yet, we held art festivals. On Mother's Day it was

Madonna and family paintings by local artists. Soon these were judged shows with the Church having the option of buying the winning painting. In time, wonderful art had a chance to grace the bare walls, stair cases, and halls of the church.

We bought three busses on the cheap: one for the nursery school, and another for the children's after school program. The third bus was used for senior excursions, such as a day trip to see the wildflowers or whatever. All of this was not without problems.

I was driving a newly acquired ex school bus with every seat taken with adults. We were on our way to the Nethercutt Museum. A car stopped short in front of the bus. I of course slid rubber. No problem there, but while going through a heavy industrial section the tread on the left front tire flew off. You guessed it, no jack, and no spare and it being Sunday, every office in the area was locked up. Cell phones had not been invented. No traffic and no air conditioning. Every uncomfortable school bus seat was filled with adults sweating and muttering something about lynching being too good for me, etc.

I valued the stained glass windows in the sanctuary. Each window had a figure of a person who had a major role in the history of our faith. John Wesley is there with Martin Luther. The Rose window was spectacular and unlike any other. What made it so was that near the bottom was depicted a dog. The story was that the giver of the window said either my dog is in the window or no gift of the window. Hence the window in all of its beauty and glory also honors St. Pooch.

The negative side of all of this activity was that the church did not have a real parking lot. Solution? Do some serious trading with another church who had a piece of land adjacent to our facility, for something acceptable to them. The trustees turned it down.

I found the third floor of the office and Sunday School building jammed full of items that did not sell at rummage sales long past. Clearing out all of the truck loads of "junk" which had accumulated over the years was a major task, but it made available space for youth programs, and it was very satisfying.

Entering into community life we took down every church banner and carried them in a community Christmas parade. This was well received. Then I asked the bell choir to march and play, which had never been done in the history of the parade. The crowd applauded. This was a smash hit. Earlier in Advent we found the backdrop painting used in a film depicting night time Bethlehem, and used it for a backdrop for the bell choir playing Christmas music. All a joyous time.

Christmas Eve was a special event using the park across the street and even the street, which took a police permit. With four trumpeters appearing from the parapet of the steeple, everyone stood in the street following the Christmas eve service and sang the hymns of Christmas.

Things were going so well. We were having a grand time, when we were asked or told to move again. This time it was again to another downtown church, but again with no parsonage. Did this change our lives? More than we could ever guess.

In order to move our things were piled (read dumped) on Ruth's mother's lawn at Baker Homes and we prayed there would be no rain. And then came a change I never considered in our lives or ever prayed for, but which we have been more than grateful, and now see as God's caring hand and provision by God's grace.

XIII

CHURCH # 8

HISTORY IN THE MAKING

*This congregation changed our
retirement. We now own our home.*

✳ A Historical Appointment

This Methodist church had a history. It was the first church
of any denomination of any kind in the city of Orange. It

was begun with the name "Methodist Episcopal Society," 1873. It's a story that needs to be told. So here it is.

A 10-year-old boy watched his dad take off his coat and shoes, and dive into a flooding river answering a cry for help. They both drowned. His widow could not keep the farm, so she sold it and bought a covered wagon and two oxen. Her unmarried sister joined her and with others headed west, setting off for California.

Crossing the Sierras with winter coming on, a miner took them in. Come spring, the miner and the sister got married and the widow and boy pushed on to Sacramento, California. The boy earned money by shooting rabbits and selling them door to door.

He became a lawyer, then a judge. While on a case in San Bernardino, he fell deathly sick and knew he was on his deathbed. A Methodist Pastor called on him, prayed for him and the judge recovered. The Judge then decided to be a Methodist Pastor. He was soon ordained. His first appointment was to start a Methodist Church in a spot called Richland, known today as the City of Orange.

In his journal he noted that the Santa Ana winds blew so strong, it blew the chapel he had built off of its foundations. He called for help and a group of helpers picked up the chapel and returned it to its rightful place. The spot he had chosen to put the chapel was what he saw standing up on his saddle, looking around over the wild mustard weed that covered the future city of Orange.

That spot is where the Orange UM Church now stands. This land was later given to the church by a former Confederate Captain, Henry Glassel. In the Civil War, the captain had used a steam launch with a boom extended over the bow of his command with an explosive on the end of the pole. It was with this that he tried to sink Union ships of war. He survived, earning him the title of POW. After the war, he became a land developer.

The newly minted Methodist minister I have written about here was named Rev. William Knighton, a Methodist Pastor on my list of faith heroes. He is also remembered as one of four Methodist ministers who gave their libraries and founded the University of Southern California. I need to note that his next assignment was to plant a church in Ventura, CA, which is a thriving body of faith today.

✴ Owning the Parsonage

"Ruth, look at this."

We were in a tourist shop in England. After we laughed, we bought a fine ceramic sculpture entitled "The Parsonage" (David Winter, 1984). It sits in our living room today. Technically we now owned " The Parsonage" for the first time in our lives.

A concern that was seldom spoken, but was always there from the beginning of our ministry, was now coming front and center, no longer on the back burner. Our whole ministry we had lived in provided housing. Twice we could not occupy a parsonage for some weeks and so we camped with Ruth's mother till the church could buy a house into which we could put our home.

Now we were called to serve our last appointment, and after that, it looked like we would be sitting on the curb. The God-faithful factor took over. We were asked by this appointment if we wanted money to rent or would we like to buy a house?

Buying was the desire, beyond question, but after our four children had been through college level training, it was a humorous joke. We couldn't come close to anything resembling a down payment. Then the One called Holy, spoke.

The church offered to loan us what was needed at 8% interest for a down payment. This was seen as manna gift-wrapped from heaven. We, for the first time in our lives, were under a roof where we held the title, even if it was mortgaged. We knew it was a God-sent mortgage at just the time in our lives when it was needed. Soon the market for housing started going up and up and this let us finally thumb our noses at the bank and burn those loan papers.

Ruth remodeled every parsonage we had lived in and left them better than we found them. But we had ownership now and all that it meant. After looking at most of the houses for sale in Orange County, we bought the house of the former pastor. This came with all that goes with home ownership, including coming up with furnishings.

To illustrate, we contracted for a tile hall floor. We had gone to a church function and were not home when the tile was being put down. We got home late and the tile job was done. The only problem was the tile angled off and was not square with the house by a good bit. Seems that the tile man had an adult beverage addiction.

Ruth and I looked at the clock, then took up every tile before the cement hardened and relaid the tile straight, which took us most of the night on our knees. The kicker was when the tile layer came to collect his check the next morning, he commented his tile job really looked great. Grinding my teeth, I made no comment as I handed him the check.

Sometime later I was crawling through the attic to rewire a backyard sprinkler system. I was in semi-darkness, misstepped, and fell through the living room ceiling and down through our shelves holding items that were special to us. I had time to clean up the mess before

Ruth got home from work. It was three days before she noticed the big hole in the ceiling.

One other item worthy of note was the promised three-week project of putting in a new sewer pipe. A small job, so we lived with an open ditch through the kitchen for a number of weeks, longer than the three weeks the job was supposed to take. Finally, the pipe had a plug put in it to test for leaks, the ditch was filled, the earth tamped down, the cement poured, and matching tile laid. Then the long cleanup. It all sparkled. The water was turned on. It just backed up and mocked us. Someone forgot to remove the test plug, so it had to all be dug up again and in a moment the stopper was removed.

Such is home ownership.

✳ A Real Mystery

My first issue at this new appointment was a mystery that everybody in the congregation knew what it was but me. Each Sunday morning during the service quiet time, or my sermon, I could hear a soft, somewhat faint, "click,click,clank." No one seemed concerned but me. It was almost always there if you listened. My curiosity became more intense as the weeks passed. Of course, I could not go searching for the origin of this sound as I was in the pulpit. Besides this quiet disturbance was at times intermittent.

The answer came in a roundabout way. There were two lady in-resident saints who had kept track of congregation giving since anyone could remember. They had a small locked office but they wanted to hear the newly appointed pastor. So they moved to a coat closet in the church entry narthex.

One of the doors into the sanctuary was always open. What I was hearing was their adding machine. They always left before the benediction and it was then just a closet.

Mystery solved.

✳ Labor Day: Real Work!

The big event in the community was a major food fair street event on Labor Day weekend. This was real street evangelism time. We opted to sell big drinks of ice tea. This was made five gallons at a time and sold as fast as it could be brewed.

All went well in the heat of the day but not at night. Having a brain spasm I came up with "Let's have a dunk tank." Sitting on a bench, when a well-aimed baseball is hurled right, the bench drops the pastor into the cold water. I swear this town had more major league pitchers than Brooklyn, or the Baptists saw an opportunity as I was dunked often.

What I did not factor in was that the bright lights were in my eyes and I, and those who also sat on this perch, could not see anything to get ready for the dunking. It was at any given moment the unexpected dropped you into the cold abis. I highly honor those who said they would do this crazy duty with me. I resolved to speak more about tithing instead of selling ice tea and making a fool of myself being dunked.

On the day before Lent, Fat Tuesday, there was an observance that started in Laurence, Kansas. Not being above stealing a good idea, the church sponsored a community pancake or flapjack race. Women with a skillet in hand and flapjacks flipping would race around the block. The winner was crowned with the honor of winning. It proved quite popular.

❋ Never Strike a Child

My church joy was starting a nursery school and every Wednesday having Childrens' Chapel. We sang together, and I told a biblical story on their level. Like in the previous church, because so many of the kids were from single-parent families, I again had a rule that those who wanted a hug would get one from me. They would line up for their hug; no doubt today I would be having a hard time at taxpayer expense going to court because I did this. I have never regretted nor ever been sorry for hugging those children.

There was something bad in all that was going on. Apparently, there was a nursery school teacher who was slapping the kids who didn't do as she said. This hit the fan when a mother saw this happen. A lawsuit was threatened by the child-slapping teacher's father, who was a lawyer, who said, "If you fire my daughter I will....." We could not dismiss her unless we gave her $10K, which bothers me to this day.

Hard to believe but there is more.

❋ Agree to Disagree Agreeably

The long running disagreement among the old-timers went back to the building of the present church. I was told that it was not feasible for both sides to have what they wanted. Dividing the congregation about fifty-fifty, some were for buying an organ and others wanted to install air conditioning. The organ backers won, so I was told it was a closed issue when inquiring about looking into air conditioning.

Every member was well aware of how hot the building

became in summer. I already talked to a former member who was now the mayor. I probed about getting trees planted on the street side of the sanctuary for shade.

The Mayor thought I implied we would pay for them and to be certain it was done right, he went ahead with city crews to do the job. I had no funds or permission for trees. The city paid for the trees and my friendship with the Mayor was thin from then on. Besides, I found that all the electrical for air conditioning had been installed when the building was built. Adding it was a snap. Grumbling and brow perspiration stopped.

✳ Taking Brides for a Ride

Having been heavily infected with the admiration of autos of yesteryear, I restored a vintage somewhat, mostly, 1915-17 Buick out of wrecks of mixed heritage and odd parts. I then offered to take adventurous couples for whom I had just performed the knot-tying ceremony to go to their wedding reception in my vintage Buick. This was often the case as we had a 'no alcohol' rule on church grounds. Almost all accepted this ride and it was fun for them and me.

Once, waiting at a red light, a Bentley also stopped at the same light. The male in the backseat rolled down the window and asked, "Have you any Gray Poupon?" (No one under thirty will understand this, but the bride and groom did and the Best man added it to his toast (and most of their guests got it). A good laugh was had by all.

My wise wife pointed out that it would be smart to have insurance. Cheapest I found was taxi insurance at eight grand a year. I did take a few more couples but prayed a whole lot more along the way for Divine assurance, or a very alert angel riding along.

✳ An Unbelievable Wedding

The start of this story is off the scale of believable. It happened as my caregiver and I were eating breakfast. Because he had worked as a roustabout in the oil fields and I had worked for Refinery Maintenance, we had stories that needed telling. This one takes the cake.

Thinking about this wedding. I asked him if he had ever heard about the bride I am now writing about. She had a TV series. He responded, "Sure, we lived next door to her best friend."

It was a wedding straight out of Hollywood to take place in a plush coastal hotel. After the drive to get there, I held the rehearsal and then Ruth and I joined the wedding party for the rehearsal dinner. The groom was in a popular rock band, so his best men/ushers were all musicians. The bridesmaids were Hollywood beautiful like the bride.

Ruth and I were seated next to the bride's father and mother. Next to Ruth was the rancher dairy farmer brother of the groom, who told her that "if any boy dressed like my brother came to the door to date my daughter, I'd boot him clear across the street." This is an exact quote.

Next morning we had to leave our room at 11:00 a.m., so I put my best clerical garb in a room shown to us for visiting clergy, then we treated ourselves to "High Tea." This was an experience new to us both, and "most elegant." The cookies were so small I had to be careful trying to pick them up. Other than that, it was an elegant life moment.

Time moved along saying it was a good idea to get ready. We returned to the room where we stashed my wedding garb, and found the room bare, clean and empty. The staff had not a clue what had happened to my wedding robes. They searched the hotel. Nothing.

Finally they called a Roman Catholic Priest, and produced a robe shorter than me by a lot, and not too clean. It looked ridiculous on me. Meanwhile, neither bride nor the groom were ready.

At the last moment, the father of the bride from the previous wedding appeared with my wedding garb saying, "This is not ours." I said with clenched teeth, smiling, but with a lot of relief, "You are so right." I then truly welcomed him royally. Ruth helped me put on my robes and my world was once again in good order.

I need not have hurried, as we were told the bride was not yet dressed. This message was repeated off and on for an hour. Meanwhile, security people were sorting out the wedding crashers from those with an invitation.

A plane flew low over the area, throttled back, and a man dressed in a tux with a magnum bottle of Champagne in hand parachuted out of the plane. He landed on the putting green with both heels forward, leaving two furrows across the green, followed by indents where he bounced. Never heard if he had an invitation. I would not be surprised if he is still making payments on fixing that putting green.

Ruth tells about her being taken into the groom's family. She, being the friendly type, had a good time talking with the wedding party at the rehearsal dinner. When the wedding was finally ready to begin, she stood at the back because there were no seats. A groomsman noticed her and insisted she come with him; he took her to the front row where she was seated on the groom's side next to the groom's brother. She became an instant great aunt.

It was a black and white wedding, with the audience divided into white on the bride's side, and black on the groom's. Only the bride and groom wore white, he in white leather and she in form-fitting white. She could not go up the three steps to the platform without jumping to do so.

After the ceremony came the usual business of taking wedding pictures, but they did not take any of the "aunt" no one could quite place. Next came the party, food, dancing, and we left.

I had some 30 years in Rotary and attended my Rotary meeting the following Thursday. It was a normal meeting with a few who had gotten their names or picture in the news or newspapers being fined, which is the usual practice. I sat low in my seat, and at the close, I was home 'Scot free.'

Little did I know that our President always read the National Enquirer after the Rotary meeting. The wedding was the whole centerfold, and I was his big fat target at the next Rotary club meeting. I helped raise the budget of our club from a good chunk of our family income with a fine. It all goes to a good cause: eliminating Polio world-wide, so no resistance from me. All a part of a service club life.

It was while serving this church that The Orange Rotary Club asked me to lead a Group Study Exchange Team to India. My team would be made up of four young businesswomen. I suggested my (Ph.D.) wife go along with me and all agreed that it was a marvelous idea, so Ruth got to be a part of this unique adventure, with Rotary picking up the tab. It was an experience and memories that we share. (See Part Two.)

※ Music for the Soul

Seeking a gifted choirmaster is something best left to others. When the local high school choral director led our choir, I noted several high school student strangers appeared in the choir. That day I set about having him as our Choir Master. In time he became that, along with the kids who followed him. It was a win-win.

Two and a half miles due West was The Crystal Cathedral and Rev Bob Schuler. Anything we did, he was doing in spades, spotlights and all done with an expensive flair. One morning he had fifty caged singing canaries upfront announcing spring. I just announced it. In truth, if the Cathedral had a chill, we had winter.

Our organist was on staff at the Cathedral, but It wasn't for him to play the organ. It was for him to draw up the plans for every guest speaker and each and every other person to be told where to stand, and at what time. Every movement calculated was the goal. He played the organ quite well for us on Sunday morning. The organ was good enough that the local college was using it as a teaching instrument, which covered maintenance costs.

Quite by accident, I got another inside look of the inner workings of this nationally known TV church. Our musical son, Tim, was in a marimba orchestra, invited to play in the Cathedral service. They met and rehearsed on a weekday evening, and then recorded the music. Though they played on Sunday morning, they were not miked. Their perfectly recorded music was what was heard on the national broadcast.

We moved the sound controls in our church up to the balcony, which I thought was rather crafty as the sound operator could see the whole congregation and better monitor the sound. If an adult was turning knobs on the board, it worked as planned. If a teen male was there, so was his girlfriend, and all expectations for following written plans for the service were gone.

Six years had whizzed by and this church was used to the pastors moving on after five. The Pastor Parish Committee vote was 50-50, but leaving it up to us to stay or leave. We had a grand celebration of ministry at the church and I hung up my robe with a lot of memories.

Frankly, I was burned out. Thirty-nine years of church wrangling made retirement mighty enticing, but to do that I needed 40 years of service, so Ruth and I went to see the Bishop. This wise man advised a sabbatical to rest up, then "you've got another church in you." I wasn't sure about that.

There was the question of money: no church, no salary. At least we had our home and a house to put it in. While we were In India, Ruth had been appointed Acting Associate Vice President for Extension Programs at Cal State U. Fullerton. Most money she ever had made, so I settled into a year off and she supported us. What a difference a year made. Decision time came around and I retired, 40 years accomplished. Ruth followed in October when she turned 62 and could draw Social Security.

We were free, and we were put out to pasture together or as St. Paul said, we were now on the shelf. At 63, I entered into the state of "superannuated" (retired but still can be called on, which happened). We gave thanks for all that our Creator had blessed us with over the forty years, as we lived out the greatest story there is.

With a solemn promise to myself and Ruth, I was NOT going to flunk retirement, and so we turned the page to see what God had for us next. Now for the fine print details that followed.

XIV

SABBATICAL AND RETIREMENT

❋ You Did What?

We got a house sitter and for eight months slowly wandered hither and yon about the U.S. in our RV. On the trip we stopped in Colville, WA, to see some mighty good friends, Lee and Louise Stevens. These were much appreciated lay people who did yeoman work in our last church, and who pushed for this book to see the daylight of ink.

They, knowing we were footloose and fancy-free, asked us to meet their friend, a realtor. Sneaky, but it worked. Only out of courtesy did we say yes. He asked Ruth to draw the layout of the ideal house. She did. He said he knew where that house was. He was right and we bought this underpriced incredible brand new house in three days... No escrow. We just needed to get a lawyer and sign the papers.

We called each of our four with this news, and there was stunned silence, then an explosive exclamation, "YOU DID WHAT?" It was at fire-sale price and way beyond anything we could begin to buy in Southern California. Plus it was on ten acres of old-growth pine trees with a thirty-mile view. Then it was back to SoCal to sell our house, pack our goods, and head north.

And so it was that we retired to the NE corner of the State of Washington with benefits, never hazarding a guess what those benefits were as we left So Cal. First, it was like turning back the clock to 1955. Very few locked their houses and car keys were in the ignition or on the seat. I was soon a member of the Juvenile Court where the serious indictments were shoplifting lipstick, etc. It took time to get used to this different world and we liked it. No, we loved it.

Having been a member of a service club and the Ministerial Association (MA) through most of my ministry, I soon joined both. Rotary was as expected, but the MA was awesome. The town was small and isolated so there was only one church of each denomination.

For me, they soon became like extended family. The central concern was the community, and working together was ideal. The best of all of this was that none of us got away with anything. We had two Roman Catholic Priests and three nuns who were rather quiet (or they could not get a word in edgewise). There were seven churches involved and no one missed our monthly meetings for anything short of a funeral. It made each of us pull up our theological socks.

As the trust level grew, we all owned up to having had a few hard-headed parishioners, and a lot of saints, at one time or another. Each noted having had either a saintly secretary or one, for good reason, wished we never had. I called one of mine behind her back, "Warden," but the rest were hard-working gifts called sweating Saints.

I asked a lot of questions and learned a lot. When one of the RC Priests in our group was killed falling asleep at the wheel, I was invited to participate in the Mass at his funeral and I could say, "good friend, deeply respected." He was the one who quietly said, after I had made a statement,

"The only one we are absolutely certain is in heaven is the thief on the cross beside Jesus, as our Lord turned his head and said, "This day you will be with me in Paradise." I could only acknowledge that he was right. This very special ministeral group presented me with a handmade stole which they all signed when we left, and it is still treasured.

Not serving a church, I was asked to fill in on Sunday for a good personal friend. He was the Sr. Rector of the Episcopal church, and he asked me to bring the sermon. I prepared for the Homily of the Day the text called for. He followed the High Church Formal Liturgy. When it came time for me to speak the Word, I stepped out from behind the altar and did not go into the pulpit, but rather stood out front as was my custom. Pointed out to me later, this was never done. One of their Executive Committee had a heart-attack just as I was about to speak. I never got to utter a word of what I had prepared, and they never asked me back.

One surprise was unexpected as Ruth had made a donation to public radio, and they thanked her on the air. A friend was listening who had moved from our last church and lived in the area. She quickly called Ruth. The reunion was fun, and as our friends were amateur paleontologists, we joined them as a family of faith. We also joined them on old bone hunts in the hills.

I found out that this friend had bought a retired school bus, filled it with cut wood, backed it up to their own back door, and never went outside all winter to get firewood for their fireplace. They quickly became friends of the first order.

At night we could see one light which was some ten miles away across the valley, but also an uncountable vast number of stars. In the spring the hills were rejoicing with lavender lilac blooms, making it postcard beautiful. It was a special time in our lives.

Following are two more examples of retirement, before I close this story.

Making blood donations at a picnic

✳ To the Arctic Circle

Retirement meant time to take a long dreamed of vacation trip in our RV to see Alaska. It began with a major oversight. We spread out the maps under our dim lights in our dining room. What was not noticed was the road we chose to take had intermittent red gaps, which meant driver beware, use at your own risk.

Taking this road meant we saw a lot of wildlife, and a day's travel meant we met very few if any, fellow travelers. We camped alone beside awesome lakes. We drove through incredible country and pressed on. Mostly red roads on the map did mean logging roads or roads under construction or use your imagination. Such goes up the western edge of Alaska and is named the Corsair Highway.

I have other suggestions for this wilderness path. It did let us see some of British Columbia.

We saw a sign,"Next gas, 131 miles." No problem. Got there, and it was long since closed, and abandoned. We were towing a Metro Hudson I had restored and it had six gallon gas cans in it, together totalling 36 extra gallons. This augmented the 97 gallon RV tank.

I was asked often about our mileage on our 454 Chevy engine. My answer was always 14 mpg. Six in town and eight on the road...with the wind. Six and eight is fourteen. Only a few smiled. Seems those trying to be a wit, succeed by half or math was not their thing.

In White Horse, Yukon, Canada, we attended church. Great service, but it was the organist that was of interest. He was dressed ready for the beach. Tank top, shorts and flip flops. He invited us to dinner and we found his bed was on the floor by his organ, so if he awoke with an inspiration, he could capture it.

We had trouble with a new Mallory fuel pump in our RV. On any uphill grade it would cut out. I found a burr on the armature and filed it down. Problem solved.

Before this we stopped at a garage for a replacement fuel line which I thought was the problem. I found the garage owner close to tears. At a mining camp 400 miles from nowhere, his crew had installed a new generator. It went on line at 220 volts and burned out every radio, refrigerator, lamp, etc. in the camp, and all else that was wired for 110 volts in this obscure corner of the world.

We learned what frost heaves are. The road suddenly becomes a really big roller coaster. They always have black marks leading to these sudden steep valleys and hills by those who knew to look for them. Being aware, we also slid rubber as these could easily break springs an/or imprint your head prints on the ceiling of the RV.

On this road all traffic was stopped because there was a good sized river crossing the road. We waited for a couple of hours. A beaver dam had come apart upstream.

There was a C47 plane beside the road with a big hole in its side. Someone had left their lunch in the plane and a bear had retrieved it, I was later told.

In Anchorage we picked up our mail we had asked to be forwarded. Ruth for some reason returned to the post office, and found that now all of our future mail was to go to Alaska. She changed it back to our home address.

While in Anchorage we went to church. Some really good friends had been assigned here and we planned on surprising them. We soon learned there are five Methodist Churches in the city and we had no idea which one they attended, but it was not the one we went to that morning.

One problem was that the nights were incredibly short, so all the windows were covered to get some sleep. This did not shut out the revelry of those who were enjoying the sun every minute possible, with all the noise they could make.

We came across a city celebrating the 4th of July. Their main event was to put thousands of rubber ducks on a river. Each duck was numbered and a bet for a dollar was placed on that duck to reach a finish line first. In the name of my sister, I bet Guyvanna's birthday on one duck, which had an impediment of not hurrying, despite my frantic shore line encouragement.

We drove the Metro Hudson, our RV tow car, to the arctic circle just to say we had been there. Ruth laid out a grand picnic lunch. After grace we began to enjoy ourselves. Then they came, the Alaskan national bird, the mosquito. I have the memory that the majority of them had to turn into the wind to either land or assault us. We made a record setting run to our vehicle to finish our picnic memory of an interruption by blood thirsty, airborne predators, native to Alaska.

It was easy to choose to return home via the Al-Can Highway. One instance on a cliff side road had Ruth singing a hymn. On a high mountain part of the road, with a sheer drop next to us, the tow vehicle of the RV in front of us began to slide toward the edge of the drop off. Ruth began to sing "Nearer my God to Thee," then noted as she moved to the back of the RV, "This is a 25 hymn road!"

✻ One More Story

The Stevens whom we had first stopped to visit in Washington were way beyond any ordinary couple, he being a retired college president with saltwater in his veins, meaning he was an avid deep water sailor. His unlimited talent was being a classic woodworker.

She was a law professor with championship-winning skill in the game of Bridge, and an awesome hostess. Louise is the one who pushed me to write these stories down most every time we met or emailed, and I may forgive her someday.

They took us and other landlubbers on three yachts to sail the Greek Islands. But first, we had to learn the language and art of standing at the helm commanding the direction of the pointy end of the boat, at the whim of wind and current.

A feared rare sight to see, but we pulled two
frightened swimmers out of the water

The humor came when we were trying to learn to sail backward. Before you laugh, this is needed to back into a stone wharf and tie off, with spring lines. Other sailors, as we practiced this in the San Juan Straights, kept well clear of us. I'm sure they thought we had to be incredibly drunk as we floundered about learning this skill. It all came together for two weeks looking and playing like we were millionaires, a time never to be forgotten.

However, a once in a lifetime, rare event did occur. Having just put out to sea after lunch one day, we saw in the distance what looked like a boat on fire. Our three boats all headed toward what sailors fear most, fire at sea. Two men were truly in a world of hurt, diving into the water just as we reached them. They had saved just one passport and one wallet. Everything else went down with their boat. The fire started in the galley, burned their dingy that was above it, and they were fortunate to escape with their lives.

Back home, life couldn't have been better except for one thing: our family was 1300 miles away. Visiting them in the RV just wasn't enough, so on our return from sailing, we sold our dream house and most of its furnishings, packed up the rest, and headed back to sunny Southern California where we still live today, some 26 years so far, but we see family as needed.

We are truly not retired and we are not going to ever flunk retirement. We often offer our thanks to our life creator for the doors which opened up our world to the joy the pastoral ministry offered us.

PART TWO

TRAVEL AND WORK WITH TEEN AGERS: A WINNING COMBINATION

TRIP ONE:

THE BELGIAN CONGO, AFRICA

Don (seated), Lee, Gary, Jeffry, Keith, Ron
Amazing team, plus one stationed
there who spoke Swahili

✳ **Getting There...**

The annual conference of the So. Cal. MC had authorized
a work team to be sent to the Congo. The team was made

up of four college men, all tops, and myself. We were to teach Africans how to use and service the number of one-cylinder diesel tractors that many churches had underwritten as a gift to a nation coming into being. I was chosen to lead this team because I was a young pastor who also had worked with and understood diesel engines.

One cylinder diesel tractor out of many we
never saw, because of the revolution

In the Belgian Congo an African could be jailed if he put a spanner (wrench) on a bolt. That was a white man's work. We had been assigned to an agriculture station. The first item was to show the Africans the advantage of planting in rows. We were more than excited - but first, we had to get there. I had contact with an outfit that had a WWII seaplane (PBY). They would get us there at half price. Someone at the Conference Headquarters nixed that.

We were to leave on a Sunday and the UM Conference gave me a check for all of our foreseen expenses. It was delivered late Friday night. As you know, banks are closed on Saturday. The check was for over $38,000, which was money raised to send us to Africa. Getting that check cashed was an adventure in itself. Carrying that much cash was hair standing up spooky, and made me jumpy. Being able to turn that check into cash came under the heading of a minor miracle. We were now on our way.

The first stop was London with enough time there to be tourists. I booked a private tour for a quick "see the sights." I have a photo of all four of the team asleep on that bus.

Next stop, Paris, where somehow, someone suggested we climb the Eiffel Tower by using the maintenance stairs and handholds, so we did. One of the team panicked near the top. I think it was because he looked down. He was unable to neither go up or down. In order to help him, I wrapped myself around him but had to pry his hands loose. This was harder than you might think because he had what seemed to be a death grip.

No, we did not go on to the top. He is now retired, having worked for the UN, but I think he has since avoided high places. I have always wanted to check to see if he imprinted his fingerprints on that girder, but never checked it out.

Next came Athens. I had sent my passport to The Hashemite Kingdom of Jordan to get a visa, and never got it back. I found out later all of the staff were on vacation. An appeal to my Senator got me a reissue ASAP, and it was sent to Athens.

Meantime Jordan sent mine to my home and Ruth had a TWA pilot carry it on the next plane to Athens. I now had two valid passports, which had me at the center of attention at the US Embassy. They invalidated one passport by punching holes in it.

In Athens, I bought two small reproductions of 4th century B.C. Greek sculptures at the Acropolis, and I knew I now owned two treasures. More about this later.

By now we were becoming a team with our own

language. We agreed that Helen of Troy was the most beautiful woman that ever lived because her face "launched a thousand ships." By common consent, the girlfriends and my Ruth were evaluated as One Helen. The team could now evaluate female pulchritude by fractions, or by millihelens. If one of the team noted an attractive young lady and noted she was 700 millihelens, we all knew the meaning, or offered another number, and she or no one else had any idea what we were talking about. Remember the team was made up of young college men.

Then on to Uganda, and a dinner well remembered, not for the food, but for the waiters. Every one of us had our own waiter standing at our elbow. They were all coal-black, in contrast with their starched, snow-white uniforms. What was unforgettable was that they were all barefoot.

The hotel was one room with a roof made of elephant grass which harbored more living things chasing each other than I wanted to sleep under. We all bedded down under the stars.

Our plane into the Congo was vintage. There were four other passengers all wearing pitch helmets which said they were old Africa hands. At the airport, there was a long line waiting to board the plane to leave the country. That should have been a clue of what was going on, but we were excited to be in the Congo at last. Make that *very* excited.

✳ Freedom in a Box

We arrived, looked around, and it really was Africa; no doubt about it. We were taken in hand and led through customs with the officials speaking French. Quickly being pushed through the crowd, we and our luggage were crowded (crammed) into an older van, and something said to the driver, and in ten minutes we were in the bush dodging potholes and looking out of every window, with all of us talking at once.

The van stopped, we got out, and a mass of curious people greeted us. We were at "methodiste anglais" agricultural farm in Kinandu. The locals knew this place was going to become a part of the Republic of the Congo in only a few more days. This would soon be an independent country and finally out from under the thumb (exploitation) of Belgium. We were there to rejoice with this nation newly being born. It was history and we all knew it.

Sunday came, and it was 4:00 a.m. I was awakened by the grounds and the church being swept in preparation for services. The chapel had a very clean-swept dirt floor, and no glass in the rather large windows, but it had a corrugated tin roof.

I was asked to speak on this momentous occasion of freedom, and the shedding of the yoke of colonialism. Every word I had prepared was considered, rehearsed, and polished. All were worthy of the events taking place. Of course, I had an interpreter and so my very carefully chosen words were repeated in Swahili. I believe the translator said something like, "Bawana has cleared his throat, with variations."

During my oration, a boy of about 4 years old, naked below the waist, and holding onto the tail of a goat, came down the center aisle of the church. This latecomer was noted only by me. So much for the importance of my independence speech.

They knew that the laws under Belgium would be no more. For example, there was no legal education beyond the 4th grade. One exception: the 6th grade was for those going into the postal service or into a few areas of the government. In short, it was hard for us to believe how oppressive it was for these people. They had no mechanical understanding, but they learned quickly.

The day of independence was soon upon us and we all went into Elizabethville for the great celebration. The team was invited to the Bishop's home and we felt honored to be there. Unfortunately, I was a witness to a loss that the Bishop experienced, which brought him to tears.

He had a wooden bookcase with a glass front. We talked about books for a bit and he went to the case to share a commentary passage about an item in the Gospels. On removing a book, and opening it, he discovered that it was an empty hollow shell. One by one he pulled out more books, and they were like the first one.

The four legs of his priceless library were set in coffee cans filled with kerosene. The left-back leg can had rusted through and this allowed some kind of paper eating ant, to eat most of his library. He didn't cry, but it was close.

Out of kindness, he loaned me his Bolex movie camera and then handed me a Winthrop hunting rifle saying, "You may need this, considering where you are staying."

I sat down in the middle of the main street with the movie camera and filmed the freedom parade. I was impressed at how many Boy Scouts were in the parade. On the edges of the crowd, there were those selling small boxes of freedom to the illiterate. I never saw the Bishop again and on the second day of rioting, a mortar shell, uninvited, came down the chimney of what once was his home, but thank God, he was somewhere else.

That evening I saw a rather large gathering of people in an open field waiting to see a movie to be shown on a sheet. The title of the film was,"The Essence of Democracy." A speaker before the film made it clear that Communism was the best form of government. It only took a moment to recognize the film, "Grapes Of Wrath." The crowd was tittering. I asked why. The answer was they could not think of someone who owned a truck as being poor.

Back to the farm. The first thing I noticed was something I never had seen in the U.S. Much earlier than the school day began, there were kids lined up in front of the building waiting for the teacher to come.

It was while we were out gathering wood when what we saw caused us to take cover in a ditch we all dived into for cover. A group of Africans were coming our way and it sure looked like they were all carrying rifles. I had the Bishop's hunting rifle but we stayed in the ditch with our heads down for some time. It turned out the Africans were out gathering wood also. They had no guns but were afraid the sticks we were carrying were guns. Fear changes how things are seen.

Later I carefully wrapped the expensive Weatherby hunting rifle in an oilcloth and put it in a concrete pit. Knowing where it is, I can have someone retrieve it someday, was the thought. I knew I could not pull the trigger on another mortal. I figured that I could be shot if I had such a weapon in hand, meeting an armed person who was scared or had bad intentions.

❋ A Dirty River Ran Through It

Finding none of the tractors that we were sent to maintain, or to teach care and maintenance, we asked what we could do that they needed, or wanted to be done. A unanimous response was for a bridge that would not wash out each rainy season. This was a big request, and we drew up a plan for what would be needed in supplies, help, and means. Men showed up hearing this could be done. Tools were appearing, and supplies, meaning this could happen.

The bridge became the focus of our effort. The river was low and this allowed two dry islands for us to build cofferdams. A hole was dug in the center of each till we reached bedrock. Then we built in that hole two supporting rock and cement pillars with such scrap iron and steel as we could scrounge.

We only had one good diamond-tipped drill for the hardwood holes needed, and it was accidently dropped into the deepest part of the river. It had to be retrieved. The hesitation came from never drinking or bathing in river water. It was infected with bilharzia, a worm that enters the body and in time reproduces itself. It was the children we most often would see with the worms crawling out of the corner of their eyes, which was hard not to forget.

The team voted, and I was chosen to dive for the drill bit. They said I spent so little time in the water I came back up dry! I was motivated. We used beautiful hardwood for the construction of the bridge and bolted the boards together. We were told that in the following rainy season the river flowed over the bridge, but left the bridge still standing. This was also confirmed after a number of flood seasons. Our amateur efforts were good enough.

Relating this bridge-building effort to a reporter when I got home, I said, "To the team, it was like the Golden Gate Bridge in San Francisco." She headlined her story that the five of us had built a bridge in Africa equal to the Golden Gate Bridge. Since then I have been very, very careful about what I say around reporters who print their stories while buying their ink by the barrel.

✳ Hatching Advice

Our day began at sunrise on the mission agricultural station. It was basically run by Africans, and missionaries, in that order. Noting each morning when I got up, I was a bit taken back by the perfect lines of termite droppings on our beds and floor. The brown lines were directly under the wooden framework of the rafters overhead. One more thing to note about Africa was that the termites were well-fed, healthy, and determined.

Breakfast was either manioc or manioc, but always some kind of root. The manioc always served we were told was poisonous, but I was assured that the poison was squished out, or I truly hoped it was. If they didn't eat any, neither did we, but it seemed to be their staple. It sure wasn't ham and eggs or even Wheaties.

Showing off to the Africans about how much we could teach them, I got my comeuppance big time. My childhood experience goes back to pre-freeways. We lived on a dirt street and raised chickens and rabbits as well as an orchard of fruit trees. Every spring Mom would buy two trays of fifty-day-old chicks. My job was thereafter to feed the chicks, and clean the chicken yard and nests.

When the time came, I gathered the eggs, and when they were larger than pullet size, I would sell them door to door on an egg route. The sales pitch that I used, because the eggs were brown, they were whole wheat eggs.

Now in Africa we built a box, put three coal oil lamps in the bottom, and a temperature gauge at the top. Showing the Africans modern technology, we would incubate a large number of chicken eggs at one time and bring the process into the 20th century. It takes 21 days, plus or minus, for the eggs to hatch.

I marked a calendar, turned the eggs twice a day, and all of this was watched with great curiosity even by some from some distance away. This the wonder of the white man's know-how to dispense with the need of sitting hens and was attention-getting. All of this was something never seen before.

As the time neared for hatching, it was intensely watched by the Africans. There was quite a gathering and chatter on day 21, but no newborn chicks appeared. Then came day 22, then strange looks from our African friends on through day 30.

What the Africans knew that we didn't know was that the hens had never been with a rooster. So much for being a smart American and 20th-century technology which could not change the facts of life. We lost a lot of street cred in their eyes and it took some time to build back any trust.

✳ Riots Rule

Life at the Ag station went on even with our seeing smoke from burning buildings as rumors of riots became common, but nothing happened to the Ag station. The occasional gunshots heard were not rumors and had us all on edge. School had its students lined up each morning waiting for the teacher. We made ourselves busy doing what needed to be done, but this had us on alert.

In Elizabethville we had three A-3's, three young ladies who had volunteered to serve 3 years teaching how to care for and raise healthy babies, etc. By radio, we called them to come to the agricultural station for their safety. They had a small van. They brought with them what they said was their most valuable item, a kerosene powered small (think tiny) refrigerator. It was lying on its back, and stuffed with their clothes. Everything else was packed tight.

Soon they were asked to use the ice cube tray to make ice cream. It did and a smidgen was given to an African young man which caused him to shake, as he had never experienced anything that cold in his life.

✳ **Maggy**

She knew I needed my glasses;
that's why she took them!

She had to have been someone's pet. Small, with big eyes and a mischievous soul. For whatever reason she adopted me and I named her Maggy. That seemed to be a perfect fit for my new friendly imp of a monkey. I truly believe that the team took more pictures of me climbing a tree, trying to rescue my glasses that Maggy had absconded with. She would happily swing from limb to limb in the high trees. It took fruit in hand, later offered to her, to get my glasses back. Friends do such things.

I had to leave for a couple of days and when I returned I asked where Maggy might be. All was quiet, until someone said they had eaten her. She was meat and meat was expensive. Such was life in Africa.

✳ A Gun in My Face

My most vivid experience came at a roadblock. Five Africans stepped out of the bush and surrounded the car I was driving. One had a 1935 Thompson sub-machine gun poked in my face. It was the same make and model as the one I had over my desk in the Atlanta prison. The barrel was thrust through my driver's window and he said something I either could not translate, or I mentally froze. He jabbed me in my face with the barrel of the gun and spoke much louder. No, I could not find any words to say in English or Swahili.

Then I heard myself say, "Methodist Anglaise." He drew the weapon back, then motioned for us to go on. I honestly think to this day that I did not say those words, and if I had, they would have been as shaky as I was for some time after. I could see he had the safety off.

✳ The Mailman Cometh

It was a stroke of real luck or a major blessing dividend. I came across an abandoned Belgian motorcycle that no one claimed. Of course, it would not run. The fix was easy as the carburetor was the only thing that was fouled up. It was one cylinder, two-cycle, and was a real dirt bike. Riding my new found toy, I could launch off of the smaller ant hills trying for distance, and then straddling this two-wheel chariot of fire, I knew I could go where I wanted. The locals started calling me "Mwanariadha" which means "athlete". Later I learned it can be understood to mean "crazy one."

Having not heard a word about Ruth traveling cross country with our three youngsters to see her folks, I was worried. I had upgraded most everything in the old Ford station wagon but I still had concerns that old Henry Ford did make walking a pleasure. Then the word was passed on to me that there was one letter in the Mission mailbox in Elizabethville. I was off immediately to get that letter, whether it was for me or not.

I had a high level of anxiety. Could it be news from Ruth? The Elizabethville Post office stood in the center of the town square and all of the personal individual mailboxes are external to the PO with a glass front and can be opened any time.

I parked my found wheels some distance from town, by laying it down deep into the elephant grass, and walked the rest of the way. The town was almost totally deserted and all the stores were closed and secured mostly with iron doors. I walked slowly and in the shadows, not knowing what to expect. Everything seemed too quiet as I checked out the Post Office.

I started to walk over to the Mission mailbox and a car backfired, or so I thought, but dust kicked up by my foot and I suddenly knew different. I then hunkered down in the Post Office wing, reached up and opened the mailbox, grabbed the envelope, and ran. I was never good at broken field running but my coach would have applauded my agility going back. Yes, there were more shots, but I dove into a safe niche between two buildings, despite the howl of protest of the man already holed up there, whom I had not seen when I piled into him.

He was an Arab who spoke no English, but we soon decided it was best if I stayed put. Then without words, it was accepted we would wait till dark to move on. The firing was so wild that I knew the snipers were drunk. I think this was the moment I first said a prayer of thanks for alcohol.

My new Arab friend had an ivory carving and being that English and Arabic numbers are the same, we bartered the hours away. I paid him when at long last, night darkness came. We both crawled for a distance, then I ran, found the bike and took my life in my hands, having no headlight, and tried to return to the place I left that morning. A thought you do not want to entertain in the dark in Africa is how many noises in the bush are carnivorous.

Yes, I had opened the letter, and yes it was from Ruth, and everyone without a doubt at the Mission would be interested in what my Ruth had to say. I have asked her to tell her story now.

Ruth talking now:

While Lee was looking for mail, I was driving our three young children across the U.S. to spend the summer with my parents in Michigan, not realizing that Lee was not receiving any of my letters. Somewhere in the prairie states, the wiring in the motor caught fire. I grabbed the kids, set them on a dirt mound by the road, and smothered the fire with the youngest one's blanket.

What to do? I hailed a farm truck. The driver used the wire that held down our luggage to fix the engine wiring, and I decided it would be wise to stop over at my grandmother's in Kentucky. A couple of days later all the dials in the instrument panel laid over, so I was very happy to arrive.

My "Nannie" asked me to get her some medicine from the town center drug store. There I saw a greeting card, giggled, and thought how fun it would be for Lee to receive it in Africa. But my Nannie would certainly not approve of it, so I went back to her house without it. It nagged me. Finally, I returned, got some Green Stamps with it which I put in the card, and mailed it.

The front of the card was a cartoon floozie, overweight, stockings turned down and a big flower in her hair, with these words, "Hey, Big Boy...". Inside? "You forgot your Green Stamps!" I signed it, "Love, Ruth." Not a word about where we were or how things were going.

Despite having sent him numerous letters, this was the only mail Lee ever received from me all summer, and the mail he was shot at trying to retrieve.

Lee: What could I do when every person wanted to know what Ruth said besides show them the card and Green Stamps...

※ **Making Bricks**

The Africans had been making sun-dried clay bricks for some time. They added to the soil what had once been ancient ant hills, that seemed to work as a binder with the elephant grass. They piled the bricks up a certain way which seemed strange to us. They kept doing this till it was way over our heads and we didn't have a clue, but they knew what they were doing as this was their way.

They told us that now they were ready to fire the bricks.

This would take eight days and seven nights. The huge pile of beautiful hardwood they had gathered, affirmed their intentions. They waited for the afternoon wind and lit the fire beneath this huge pile of mud bricks and the fire went in and around the bricks. It wasn't until dark that we could see just how intense the fire was. It almost always needed being fed and we tended to its demands.

We had shifts, but in the early morning hours of the second day, it just got boring. The Africans danced and after a bit, they offered to teach us. With the drums and what seemed just their jumping to the sound of the jungle drums, it was simple enough. Not sure if I was inhibited or just clumsy, but it made the hours pass.

Then they asked us to teach them one of our dances. The only one we all knew was "The Virginia Reel." They had no concept of "bowing to your Partner" or "Doe-C-Doeing," so in the firelight we had no drums but lots of laughter by all of us.

They watched us do what we were trying poorly to show them, but it didn't take. They went back to drums and pounding the ground with their feet and we tended the fire. Eight days later they had a handsome pile of red hot bricks.

※ Time To Go

Things were getting no better so our 3-year women missionaries repacked and left Africa. We knew for sure they understood the situation was serious because they left the kerosene refrigerator behind. We were glad and sorry to see them go. The team had given them a rating of 700 to 950 millihelens.

The big issue was, when and how do *we* leave?

Back in town, I undertook to get an old Chevy station-wagon running. I took off the head, and did a quick valve job and all else as needed. Parts were a snap as there was no one to even lock the doors of the parts store, and it wasn't looted because what were they to do with the stolen parts? I inventoried what I took, then I left a note with my name, and the Mission's name, so they would know who had done this part self-help. After two days and an all-nighter, the old set of wheels ran like a champ.

We loaded up and hit the road south for Rhodesia. I say road; in reality, it was a high berm with two asphalt strips on top. One of the team drove and I faded out in the back seat. Whenever it was, we had entered the area of British influence, namely the nation of British Rhodesia, who have historically driven on the wrong (left) side of the road. A cement truck came into view, I was later told, who moved to the one strip to drive on and the other wheels over on the side of the berm in the dirt, as he was supposed to do when he met oncoming traffic.

Our team driver, being an American, reacting, did the same. The cement truck corrected too late. This meant it was going to be headlight for headlight. The cement truck's front wheel came up over our car's hood. This popped the car doors open and ejected the crew. No one was hurt but the African driver ran away. No part of this was his fault.

These details were told to me afterward since I was in the back seat sound asleep. I had worked all night on the car. With the impact, my body was instantly pitched up and forward to face the shattered glass of the windshield coming my way. A metal ceremonial spear that had been given to me also came with the shattered glass. It hit the back of the car hard enough to bend the tip. I have that spear, and someone, not knowing the story of the bent tip, pounded it out straight.

The accident happened near a Rhodesian cattle ranch. The lady of the ranch, hearing the crash, came running. Seeing me, she told everyone that she was an old hand at patching up those who were cut up during the London blitz. Then she sat on my chest, and had me sip ammonia, "because laddie, you are in shock and it isn't good for you to pass out." I advise anyone not to sip ammonia, but it does keep one awake. She then swabbed my face cuts with the same, and taped all the cuts down. It has healed clean and no scars. In an instant, I was no longer the team leader but the slowest one.

The country of Rhodesia did not know what to do with us. They had no category for what to do with refugee Americans. This morphed into us becoming guests of the Rhodesian government. We lived high at the government expense, in a high-class hotel with dining included.

Bandaged up, later I had an African begin to walk beside me. Looking straight ahead he said, "In the Congo, they hurt you. Here we will kill you." He never turned his head or glanced at me. One lady clerk rushed out of a store and gave me a cane I still have. As she handed me the cane she said, "Is that what they did to you in the Congo?" It was a time to remember -- the good was mixed up with the bad.

※ A Firey Moment

From some source, we acquired a vintage VW bus and were now free to do whatever we wished. It was suggested we follow the footsteps of that great Missionary explorer, David Livingston. During his career, he had only one convert, but he opened up Africa, so we started for the Zambezi River which Livingston had mapped and followed.

Africa is three times larger than the US, so there was lots of ground to cover. We camped on our way, which meant making one's bed on the ground among the elephant grass as the world turned dark. This we did, but the night sounds were stranger and louder than usual or imagined. Prudence called for remaking my bed inside the bus. I found that when I resolved to do this, every member of the team was already in the bus and fast asleep.

David Livingston discovered Victoria Falls on the Zambezi, and named them after the Queen of England. He wrote in his diary, "Angels must pause in their flight when they behold this sight." I could only agree. It is a wonder of the world of nature. We camped with a view and could only marvel at the sight of the falls.

I got a lesson in life here. An African had wood carvings spread out on a blanket for sale. I admired but was only interested in practicing my Swahili. We bartered but no price was low enough for me to buy. Under his breath, I heard him say, "I like to eat meat also." I bought several of his carvings at his top price. Guilt is a strong motivator. I did not buy the ebony ones, as I found they were made black with shoe polish.

At the fall's airstrip, I found a relic of a WWI airplane. It had WWI liberty engines, exposed rocker arms and all. Found the pilot-owner, and so sitting in wicker seats we took flight. The surprise was that in the 30 mph wind over the falls, when he throttled back, the plane stood still and I got some fabulous pictures.

Southern Rhodesia still did not know how to categorize us so we were their guests again. In a very posh hotel, we found we were welcome and, borrowing proper clothes, we were admitted. We traded our information about the revolution in the Congo. We "bush rats," as we were daubed, had borrowed ties, evening coats, and enjoyed very different food than what was normal fare beside the road as we camped. One of the team looked at the menu and said, "That will do," indicating every single thing on the menu. On my word, he ate all that the waiters brought and the government of Southern Rhodesia picked up the tab.

Somewhere later where we were camped, I messed up big time. I had no idea how gasoline got on my pants, but sitting by our campfire, suddenly my trousers were on fire. Until this, I would have bet I knew what was the right thing to do, but for some insane reason, I started to run. Keith tackled me and rolled me in the dirt.

The team packed up and started looking for medical help for my burned legs. They found a Mission doctor later that night and he did what he could. I remember two things: the Doc shaking his head saying if they get infected they will have to come off, which got my total attention.

The other item was the lighting provided by a gas-driven generator that operated at 20 cycles, which meant bright light, then fading almost to dark 20 times a minute. I recall I promised myself to do what I could to upgrade that system. No, I have not, as I have no idea where this happened.

My burned legs changed everything and the team split apart. Because of the unrest on the continent, I felt it best for the team to find separate ways home. I was put on a plane for Egypt where I might get medical care. Two found their way to Europe and on to the US, and two stayed for a bit and then traveled on home.

✳ Finding My Way Home

In Cairo, I asked a taxi driver to take me to a cheap hotel and I think he overdid it. I wanted a shower and no one would argue the need. A taxi driver knew just the place, and he was more than right. It was on the second floor over a very noisy factory and warehouse. I was glad that my room had a private shower. On the back of my room were the instructions for the shower use.

The fine print said to push my bed out into the hall as the shower head was in the center of the bedroom. What it did not say was to really tighten the on valve because it dripped. Do this before pushing the bed back into the room. This was accurate information. I now name this "tourist" hotel lest someone reading this is also taken to it while visiting Cairo: it is the "Green Nile." This is fair warning and notice.

I made another mistake I have yet to figure out. I tipped a gorilla of a man who had shown me to my room, as is our custom. The hotel manager came with this knuckle dragger and mouth breather to my room. I am not sure what he said, but I figured it was dangerous to tip as every other employee would want a tip. I never called attention to the toilet seat at the end of the hall broken into five pieces. At least this was better than the no door, brick outhouse with a hole in the floor in the Congo.

I found my way to the hospital in Cairo and a nurse named Sister Root, or in English, Sister Ruth. I knew my bride had to be praying for me and I felt my Ruth's presence as the Sister tended to my leg. I had heard of a nurse dealing with a leg going into gangrene that had a horrible smell. The patient said, "I wouldn't do your job for a million dollars." The nurse responded, "Neither would I."

My legs did not look good or smell like a rose either.

She said she could remove all of the leg skin and that there would be no scar tissue on my legs. I said go for it. She rolled the skin off both legs like a legging and bandaged them up with some kind of pungent ointment unknown to me, and I was free to go, smelling something akin to a bush animal in heat.

I got a ride in a plane going to Venice, Italy, and settled back to enjoy. The plane was soon descending into Budapest, Hungary which was behind the Iron Curtain, a country where U.S. passports are not valid. Behind "The Iron Curtain" meant don't go there.

Stepping off the plane I saw a long line of C47s. Whipping out my camera to take a picture, I saw that something was covering the lens. That something in front of my lens I tried to brush away. Looking up, it was the barrel of a rifle. I was quickly hustled off to someone behind a desk, who took my camera and passport and had me patted down. Then he muttered authoritative things and pointed to a long dark hall. At the end was a jail cell.

This I had not counted on or expected. I had read somewhere what to do, and I tried it out and it worked. Every time a guard came by, I held my breath till I had a red face, stood on my toes, and yelled "TRUMAN!"

Harry Truman was then President and someone connected the name on my passport with what I was yelling. The guards soon came running and I was put on the next plane out of there. After they returned my stuff, I looked down my nose, implying at least in my own mind, that they did not know who they were messing with. Anyway, it felt good and I was glad it worked but most happy to depart from their hospitality. With arrogance, I stood in the door of the plane just before takeoff and took another picture.

My next break came when I was in London. I was

looking somewhat like a bushman as I did not dare shave because of the facial cuts. My clothes had been unwashed since showering in them in my bedroom in Egypt.

When I bought my ticket home and mentioned that I had escaped from the Congo revolution, at no further cost I was upgraded to first class, an unexpected event thoroughly enjoyed. Then an invitation to the cockpit.

The pilots wanted to know the latest news. I had not seen a newspaper in a long time. I am sure they were disappointed. My joy was to see the navigator take a fix from the stars and I had a host of questions that led me back to my plush seat.

There are many bits and events I have not noted. But there is one more. Ruth was waiting for me at the airport, but unfortunately didn't recognize me with a full beard, weight loss, and gimpy legs, while leaning on a cane. When she realized this strange creature was me, she hugged me anyway, to her credit. At her parents' house, our two younger children backed away, except for Mark, who was eager to have me explain all the souvenirs I had sent home that actually did find their way through the mail system.

It was a joyous reunion.

I forgot to say that as I made my way up through Africa, I had every Mission doctor I found treat my legs, just like that first nurse did. It was just the doctor in Michigan who used another method who left the only scars I have.

Now in the US, I had my 30 rolls of 36 exposures film developed of our time in Africa. Most of all were shots of the upheaval of being at the right place and time to document the ugly raw truth of the newly formed nation. Everything was being ripped apart in the destruction of a full blown revolution. There were the seven to twelve incredible lucky shots I was sure I could sell to Time magazine and /or maybe even to Life Magazine, that I was most anxious to see.

I got the film back, mostly all blank. The shutter had repeatedly jammed in my Argus C3 and in the excitement of a full blown shooting war, I did not always check to see if it was working. Too late, I bought a Nikon and it has never failed me, except now. Who uses film?

Time to return home and be a pastor to those I had left to another's care.

TRIP NUMBER TWO:

YOUTH WORK TEAM TO NORWAY/ISRAEL

The flexible team

❋ How It Happened

It was Fritz LeRoque, this God person, a layman, who opened the door for high adventure for us which made this improbable story possible. We hadn't a clue what was in store for us or the team.

Fritz had taken numerous adult work teams to Europe and was ready to take another. The destination chosen for us to do this work was a church that had been bombed in Norway, WWII. We teamed up with Pastor Charles McGregor from Camarillo MC, agreeing that he would take an adult team and we would take youth.

The team was recruited and they were excited about seeing Norway. They started to raise the money needed to do all that was planned. The winner at raising money was the young man who painted house numbers on the curb and then asked of the address folk whatever they wanted to pay. The Norway church was glad to have us and was preparing for a grand event. Nineteen teenagers and Ruth and I were prepared to enjoy every minute of all that was to be, and certainly enjoy all Norway had to offer.Then the Norwegian Church opted out as the materials needed would cost more than they could raise.

Late as it was, we had to find a place to take the youth team. Fritz said, "Go work on a Kibbutz in Israel." We had a new destination and began to pay attention to the troubles in the area mentioned on the news every day. It seems to me some parent of a team member also mentioned it from that day on, as I recall. Seems they wanted their youth back whole and were pondering the issues involved where we were now going.

Following Billy Graham's rule of "don't touch the money", the MC Conference kept all the money. The issue never considered was money marked "Norway Team," meant they had money, and the Israel Team had none. The conference treasurer was a member of the church we served, and this was soon straightened out.

One check for both teams was delivered Friday evening before we were to leave. Sound familiar? This was for multiple thousands of dollars raised by each team member

($38,500 as I recall). Did you catch the word "check"? How many banks do you know that stay open on Saturday or Sunday? A majority of the piggy banks were broken, promissory notes signed, etc, to get the cash that we had to split between the two teams, headed two different places, and we were to leave in two days. Searching everywhere to cash the check, a contractor had been paid in cash for a big job. He traded the cash for the check. Thanks, Pop!

Grateful that our air tickets had been paid for, we left from LAX and I had some of both team's money sewn into my lumpy coat and a forced smile on my face.

When we got to NY, all the males of both teams gathered in the men's room at the airport. We two team leaders got down on the floor while all males crossed their arms, closed ranks, put on their grimmest face, faced outward and we pastors on our knees began to divide the money. "How many tens can you use?" "Here is a stack of $100s, now that makes how much that you have?"

Strangers who tried to use that restroom must have figured they had stumbled into the biggest crap game going on anywhere in New York. By the time the Police came we were getting up. We were asked to turn our pockets inside out. No dice. Our coats were bulging with all the cash and the police said it was the wildest story they had ever heard, while wondering if it was the truth.

The adventure had just begun, and it can be said it got worse, much worse. And no, Ruth and I have never been to Norway, though it has always been on our bucket list.

❋ The Sea was Calm? Not!

The issue was to divest me of so much cash so we had to find a bank. The team of nineteen kept me insulated from the outside world by boxing me in on all sides as we searched for a tolerant bank.

Going into a bank en masse can raise the concern of bank tellers. All was soon explained and the team's money was turned into Danish Krones. This was long planned since the US dollar fluctuated; the Krone did not. The team budget was so tight it was a safety issue.

Now before us was the joy of boarding the ship to bear all 65 of us luxuriously across the sea. I stationed myself at the head of the boarding ramp, put my brand new Nikon lens case with three new Nikon lenses between my feet, and proceeded to check everyone's papers as they boarded. Reaching down to get the case, and to my sadness, I discovered it was gone. I was glad I had my Nikon camera hanging around my neck. And so the trip began with a twinge of regret at my loss.

Why were we going by ship? Cheaper..and time to bring some kind of inner cohesion to each team, one adult and one youth, plus a touring group led by Fritz. As we sailed down the St. Lawrence to the Atlantic with the three groups lining the handrails, we saw the wonderful scenery slide by us dressed in all of its variety and splendor. At this time we all were one happy group, with smiles all around.

That evening, our first day at sea, the entertainment was a German band. Not sure how it happened, but Ruth was invited to sing with them, and she had memorized a song in German. Later, every band member wanted to talk to her and she had no idea what they were saying, because she did not speak German. Not sure the band believed her, but disappointed, they turned away.

The sea was calm, the moon was out, and I had taken some forethought as to what to do on such an evening -- because it was July 4th. As any red-blooded American will tell you, it needed a few fireworks and I had prepared. We all gathered on the fantail and "oohed and awed" together for a brief time, and then it happened.

I had not noted the fact that we were on the burned sister ship of the SS Andrea Doria, which lies on the ocean bottom. This was screamed at me in good, clear Italian by the Captain with a good sized crew, most of which had either fire hoses or fire extinguishers in hand and fire in their eyes and hate in their heart. I did realize rather quickly this was a no-no, and was worthy of the title of "stupid American." I avoided the Captain at all costs after this.

The next item was a good-sized storm with monstrous waves. The dinner tables had hinged edges that could be raised to keep everything on the table as it slid back and forth. Breakfast was fish, head, tail, and all. I think the cooks heard about the July 4th fantail item, and figured the fish would add to our seasickness.

Because of the storm, the ship fell way behind its schedule. We arrived at 2 a.m., and the three teams went their separate ways. Where I had made our reservations months before, they had no record.

I hired a bus for our 19 and taking the word of a very sleepy clerk, I told the driver to go to Broek en Waterland to a youth hostel. We made it and woke up in the 15th century. Thatched roofs, canals, and all wearing wooden shoes. Breakfast was coffee served in wooden bowls and shaved chocolate on toast. It was eaten to the last crumb.

It was Sunday so we all went to church. Worshippers paid pew rent, and we had not paid, so we were led to a half shelf in the back of the church along the wall. This was where visitors half sat and half stood. We did, and the sermon was in Dutch, summarized by the pastor for our sake in what he thought was English. We found out later that this was the place that Hans Broecker set his famous story in his book, "Silver Skates."

We were in Holland, windmills and all. The adventure was well underway. There was still the Mediterranean to cross.

❈ A Close Look at the Cold War

We met Fritz's adult touring team in West Berlin. He had tickets for us to attend a flute concert with his team. It was not music that teens were used to hearing at a concert. "It was boring" was the mumbling I was meant to hear.

Afterward we went to a high platform where we could look over the Berlin Wall. As we watched, an arm appeared out of an apartment window and for a moment waved to us from the eastern side of the wall. We knew we were looking at a death strip, just beyond search lights, mine fields, and armed guards, etc.

The facts were that well over 100,000 citizens of the GDR tried to escape across the inner-German border (or the Berlin Wall) between 1961 and 1988. More than 600 of them were shot and killed by GDR border guards, or they died in other ways during their escape attempt. They drowned, suffered fatal accidents, or killed themselves when they were caught (Wickipedia). It was hard to just look and think what it was to be on the other side of the wall in East Berlin. We saw overhead the airlift that was supplying the needs of West Berlin.

A couple on the team, while taking a walk, found Check Point Charley and crossed over into East Berlin, looked around and safely returned. I was concerned that this would spoil the team tour the next day, arranged by an East Berlin pastor, but we were able to proceed. The city was mostly silent, with almost no traffic. We were stared at after our shoes were noted. Most of the team soon had enough, and we left.

I hung back and watched the guards inspect the cars exiting. They used a low rolling cart with a mirror and lights to look under each car, to see if some citizen was trying to escape. I started to take a picture, but a booming voice yelled "NYET!" with the authority of a hand held machine gun. Quickly I exited East Berlin. The next problem was our leaving West Berlin.

Russian armed guards boarded the bus and made each of us stand as they checked our passports and pictures. The girls had little problem, but most of the males had let their beards grow and didn't look like their passport pictures. We were told that another group had been held for several days, so we were happy that after a few hours we were let go.

We were glad to continue on our way toward Israel.

If you would like to see a piece of the Berlin Wall, it is on display at the Ronald Reagan Presidential Library in Simi Valley, California.

❋ Into Another World

After touring Europe, we boarded the ship Theodore Herzel and its ever running Sabbath elevators, and entered into what was then called "The Paris of the East," Beirut, Lebanon. It was without question all that the name implied before the conflict reduced it to what it is now.

Then into buses. I am sure that the springs had been removed and the frame welded to the axle. I even was naive enough to look for air conditioning. Off across the Syrian desert we went and I was glad no one had a thermometer.

First stop, there was a sixty-foot long, six-foot-high cement wall written in large letters and in English, "Men" at one end of the wall with an arrow, and "Women" at the other end, also with an arrow. On the other side, there was only an open desert. The Arabs had both a good laugh and classic smirks as we all returned to the bus.

The next item was something wet to drink. At the next stop, I eagerly rushed to a roadside stall to buy something like soda pop. After being assured it was a soft drink, I grabbed 19 bottles of what turned out to be warm Jordan Beer.

Driving in the constant shroud of dust from the non-paved road, we came across a single post standing in the middle of nowhere. It had on top a blinking red light. The driver did slow down a bit, but drove on. The next thing that happened was what would have made the front page of the L. A. Times. Someone yelled, "Hit the DECK." Then came the roar and the bus was almost blown over onto its side.

We were crossing a landing field and a fighter jet was landing nose up. We were testing if a bus and an airplane could occupy the same space at the same time. At the other side of the airstrip we were stopped. The driver was taken out, and much hand waving and screeching was spoken. He got back on the bus, and we, wide-eyed and silent, resumed our journey.

A word about our aggressive bus driver. First, the bus had five horns. Used together I felt they could peel paint or move a small house. He never slowed down when we came to a village, where he used the horns with a semi-truck's authority. He had a crucifix on a chain around his neck. Whenever things were dicey, he held this clenched between his teeth. I asked him later about this and what I translated was, "I am putting pressure on Jesus."

Despite all that, we arrived safely at the Mandelbaum Gate of Jerusalem on the Jordan side. Here were armed guards with automatic weapons. We entered an enclosure with high walls on four sides. One of the boys started to fuss and I pointed to the men on top of the walls, all with guns pointed down at us.

The big issue here was not to have the Israel stamp in our passports. To do so would mean we could not enter any Arab country, or cross their borders. We settled for slips of paper with the Israel stamp inserted into our passports. We were motioned through the gate into Israel with a sigh of relief.

On the Holy Land side, I wanted to visit the "Upper Room," rebuilt of course. We were about 100 yards from the wall when we heard gunfire. I know the sound of high caliber guns and these were serious military automatic weapons. All of us were on the ground and as flat as possible, with my feeling that the buttons on my shirt were keeping me from getting lower to mother earth. I had the kids get up one by one and dash to safer ground.

Later we found that all this was because King Hussain of Jordan had come.The military was welcoming him by diligently guarding the border by shooting into the air. This was later explained to me to my relief.

⚹ Ramat Hashofet

We were now safe in Israel and on the road to the Kibbutz with smiles of miles past and finally getting close to our purpose and goal. Now things are a bit fuzzy in my recall, but what is not clear is how or why we somehow were taken to Jerusalem. It could have been that a bus was sent for us or?

Arriving in Jerusalem, we saw a group of dignitaries, and these men seemed to be awaiting our arrival. What I sorted out later was that with Harry S. Truman as President at that time, I being a Truman, they had moved me up in our family tree structure to be the nephew of the President. There was the Truman Point 4 Plan which was a leg up for Israel. The President was quite popular so we got lots of official welcomes.

Speeches were made, most of which uttered in Hebrew, but one thing was clear: we were guests of the Israeli government, like it or not. This meant a bus was provided to take us wherever we wished to go. I had a list that I had written earlier and handed it to the driver. He looked at it and proceeded to take us where he thought we *should* go.

The first stop was the museum of death. In the whole afternoon, we were not taken to any place I had on the list which I had so thoughtfully pondered. So much for gifts of state and politician's promises all usurped by a bus driver with his own agenda.

We got to the Kibbutz quite late, after dark. Every member of the Kibbutz, I believe, was gathered outside and all were sitting on stadium risers. They had waited so long under the stars that the night was fast turning chilly. There had been no agreement as to our time of arrival. What they knew was that it was a short drive to get there and we were late.

There were a few, terse words of welcome spoken.They had a film in a projector ready to be shown. There were few if any friendly faces. Front row seats had been saved for us, the lights went out, we found our way in the dark to the saved seats, and the projector was turned on.

The name of the film was "The Hustler" played by Jackie Gleason as Minnesota Fats, his part being a billiards player. It was a picture depicting the hard, ugly side of the world of playing pool for money. Players taken out back and their hands or fingers broken.

I had five Kibbutz elders later confront me, asking why the US would allow such films to be available around the world when they knew life depicted in the US was not as the picture presented.

They later also confronted me with what they called propaganda. This was the Chamber of Commerce slide set from the city of Redlands, California. One Truman Tripper who lived there had brought the set of slides with him. Front lawns of grass were totally unreal to them.

We were quickly briefed on Kibbutz life. Up at five, in the fields by 5:30 a.m., breakfast was brought to us at 6:30 a.m., which was always yogurt and a hard-boiled egg. Back to work, lunch in the dining hall. More often than not yogurt, hard-boiled egg, and whatever else was being harvested. Once in a great while, we had a small square of ice cream on a stick, which suspiciously tasted like yogurt.

The team had their work assignments. One was in the orchard picking fruit. I am sorry to say that one member of the team carved a swastika in the skin of an orange which caused an upheaval I had a hard time controlling. I think almost all those in the Kibbutz had the tattoo the Nazis had marked them with in the concentration camps. Only hard, steely eyes greeted me. This was no joke to the kibbutzniks. This was dealt with in our evening "ironing board" session, where hurt feelings, misunderstandings, and all wrinkles of the day were "ironed out".

My assignment was to harvest sunflower seeds. First, we cut the heads off and put them face down to dry out. These seeds I was told,were a cash crop worth $550 a ton.

I asked to be excused from work and went into the city of Mount Carmel to purchase the item that seemed to cause almost swooning, that is, chocolate. I bought the largest Swiss chocolate bars I could find and caught the next city bus back to the Kibbutz.

The bus was beyond being jammed and so I was standing. I was close to a teen, good looking, and dressed in her army uniform. She had a number of decorations and I asked her what they were for. I only remember one she pointed out, that was for garroting. If you do not know what that is, be grateful.

The team knew that I had gone to town to buy chocolate bars and a couple even ran to greet me on my return. My high moment. That evening we had a circle on the floor under one dangling dim light bulb. At the end of ironing out the team wrinkles, I handed out the chocolate bars. They did not begin eating their own chocoholic bar, rather they broke off a piece and gave it to the one seated next to them. There was a holy hush during this time until someone screamed, and then another and another shrilled the air, till all made the same discovery.

The bars were full of worms. I, in dumb innocence, had bought them on the sunny side of the street.

✳ Becoming Kibbutz-Nicks

Kibbutz life was different in several ways. Family units lived in small cottages but shared a common dining room. The 'store' used no money. If you needed something it was given to you, but only as much as you needed. Work was assigned by ability, and afternoons were saved for family time. It was true communal living in which all participated.

One item that was very different in that I had not seen anything like it anywhere, was the "Child House." A mother giving birth had six weeks for rest and did nothing else, including, if she chose, tending her baby. There were those who had been trained in baby care who took care of every need of the newborn when or if Mom chose not to. A buzzer sounded if the child was hungry and a nursing Mom could choose to not nurse.

After six weeks she was assigned an easy job like folding laundry. If she chose to never see the baby, it would be raised by those who were trained to raise the child.

The fallout of all of this was that those who were potty trained together would not date each other when the time came. I heard, "She is too much like my sister." As the evening shadows fell, there were Ford tractors heading out to go to other kibbutzim, with the driver having a glint in his eye his "sisters" never saw.

I noted that strapped to the inside of the right rear fender of each tractor was a 1935 Thompson submachine gun, which did not detract from the moonlight with romance in the air. Interesting to me was that kibbutzniks were only 8% of the population, yet supplied 28% of the officers in Israel's army.

✳ Christmas Balls

Being by myself, I gifted myself.

I stood outside the 400 year old Basilica of the Nativity in Palestine, knowing it had been affirmed as the spot where Jesus was born.

This place was marked by the wife of the Emperor Constantine. He had stopped the persecution of Christians. He was not a Christian but his wife, Helen, was. Not only did Helen ask the local Christians where Jesus had been born, but with the resources of the Roman Empire, she had the building erected that now houses the grotto marking the spot.

The entry door is very low and small. Upon entering you have to bow to the altar which is at the far end of the hall. Hanging from the ceiling are a number of massive wrought iron chandeliers, circular in shape, held up by heavy chains. I was taking it all in when a Greek Orthodox Priest caught my attention. I called on my three years of Greek studies and replied as I could. He said he could speak English and so I got a personal afternoon tour beyond price, in English, with no language struggle.

He pointed out the cannon sized balls, two thirds of the way down the chains, holding the oil lamplight fixtures. He went on to say these were there to keep the rats from drinking the oil in the lamps. Then he said that when this land had been liberated from the Muslims in the 9th through the 12th century and Christians could visit the Holy Land, those who visited this church noted the oil lamps, because candles had been invented and the oil lamps were a novelty.

These ancient tourists took mementos home, which all tourists do. These were tokens of what they had seen in their visit to this place where Jesus was born. The novelty of oil lamps no doubt they remembered. They may have bought balls that some enterprising sellers had for sale.

My Mom would say "knock on wood" if what she said was iffy. This goes back to the Druids in England who believed that the god they worshiped dwelt in trees.

So my conclusion is one I have never heard or read. As pilgrims visiting the Holy Land, they could well have taken memento balls home with them as a bit of what they had seen in Bethlehem. They were unlike anything in their lives because they used candles.

Bethlehem was where the Jesus story began and it was a must on the pilgrim visit. As they told their travel stories, they had included the balls protecting the oil in the ancient lamps. These tourist mementos could then have been placed on trees as a victory token over an ancient common Druid faith, and as a Christian faith statement.

Is that why we now put balls on our Christmas trees as a reminder that we do no longer worship a god dwelling in trees?

We have an authentic faith. The Messiah has come, and He entered our world at Bethlehem.

✳ A Hanging Takes Place

An accident I had was certainly my own fault, and it caused the leadership of the team to be handed over to Ruth.

What had happened to me was as I was working on the top side of a large trailer where we were dumping the harvested sunflower seeds. I jumped off the trailer and hit one of the wheels. I landed badly. I was mostly paralyzed from the waist down. The suggestion was given to us to not go to a state hospital, but rather go to a private care facility. We did and there were fifty of us in one room. No one spoke English. The hospital bed was way shorter than I was, and they rigged a pulley and attached a rope to each foot. Tied to the rope on each leg was a bag filled with bricks.

In the middle of the first night, I needed to empty my bladder. No night call button, so with great effort I freed myself, then crawled on the floor to a fire bucket. There was no way to get back into my bed, so I settled for a baby bed which was very low. What woke me were the excited voices saying what I later learned, "The American has escaped. The American has escaped, and he didn't pay his bill." I remember I just went back to sleep till they found me curled up in the crib.

While I was in the hospital, Ruth accompanied the

team on a trip to the Sea of Galilee. What carried them on this adventure was an open stake truck. It was exciting enough that a group of Kibutzniks joined the team. Ruth was impressed with a man named Vladameer who sat next to her. He asked her, "If a Jewish woman had the responsibilities you have and her husband was in the hospital, she would be waving her hands in the air, wailing and crying. But you are calm. Why is that?"

Ruth replied she did not need to do that because of her faith in God who was with her. He replied, "I thought so."

When the time came for ending the team's stay at the kibbutz something had to be done about me. The doctors, one of which did speak a kind of English, had me held upright and put a head harness on me. Then I was hoisted up and with a man on each leg pulling down, the doctor started giving me shots in my spine and in the muscle of my back. That's when I passed out.

Waking up, I found I was in a body cast from my neck to my hips. Ruth paid my bill and we departed for the ship. I could walk or shuffle with some help. It was great going through a crowd. I now had this four-inch thick body cast (armor) and people bounced off of me, followed by a bewildered look as they checked me out. A good thing was that I never carried a suitcase the rest of the trip, thanks to our team boys.

London produced a surprise as our city tour took us to John Wesley's Chapel, where we accidentally ran into a UM Conference team; couldn't have planned that. Now it was a clear shot for home and the Israel Truman Trip was done.

It must be told that the teams met on the airplane, abuzz with their adventures, bringing the pilot to beg everyone to take their seats because he was having trouble keeping the plane level in the air!

And so... Back to Parish work.

TRIP NUMBER THREE:

AUSTRALIA

Half of this group went one way; we went another

✳ Down Under

It was the Land Down Under that sent out a call for a work team. It was no problem gathering 18 committed youth who were willing and excited to be off to Australia to do a work project. Rather than all of the details let me note a few highlights for us as we were off to another culture, country and truly a high adventure.

We landed in Fiji, where we were greeted with the awesome singing with which they welcomed us. Their four-part harmony had the sound of the small pedal organ that missionaries used, but now they just used their voices.

My personal item at the top of my bucket list was to see the baptismal font stone where years ago the missionaries were used for human sacrifice. The first missionaries were Methodist and their lives were cut short by their being sacrificed on that rock. That cupped rock is now the baptismal font in the Methodist Church of Fiji.

The island is 84% Methodist. Fritz LaRoque had a surplus shoe connection so I had been sending those shoes to the pastors here in Fiji, and so we were doubly welcomed, most wearing their Sunday best, and their 'go to meeting' shoes.

On a Sunday morning, I asked about what it meant when they beat long and hard on a hollow log drum. They told me it was the silence that followed that was the invitation to worship. It is in the silence of our prayers God hears and speaks to those who shut out the noise that we all live with. We can then hear that still, small voice that guides us in our daily lives.

They did all things possible to make us welcome. We were taken by canoe to a feast which was held on an island that had seldom seen white people before. A roasted pig was dug out of a pit and served on large leaves, followed by island dances. We danced for them and we could tell by their discussion that they thought that they were much better than our kids. I had to agree with them. When it came time to return to the original island, the tide had gone out and the canoes no longer worked, so we had to walk back in knee deep water.

As we approached our island, our guide pointed to a place, so the first girl dutifully stepped there, and promptly disappeared under the water. He was pointing out a hole. Later, wanting to see another and different island, we walked across the isthmus, picking up seashells and checking out pools holding strange creatures of the sea. That is until the tide changed, and with its froth and sound returned our footpath back to the seafloor. When I realized what was happening, I had no need to tell the kids to run, leaving me panting up the rear of the rush to beat the sea reclaiming its turf.

✳ Look Both Ways

Next was a flight to Sidney, Australia. It was different, and the first thing we all learned was to look both ways when stepping off the curb. The second item we noticed was when we attended the church we found the seating was strange. Rather disconcerting was that there was a full pew, then an empty pew, front to back which let me wonder what I had missed in seminary. We sat in one of the empty pews and after service, noting it being winter, the congregation had sat where they had a foot resting pipe which was heated and which was in every other pew.

Looking around I also noted there was an electric coin-operated meter on the wall. If you want heat, you put in your coin for so many minutes. This was also in the gym and social hall. This seemed to be 'pay for heat' or you needed to "rug up."

We visited a family and Ruth asked to use the bathroom. The host hesitated momentarily and Ruth was shown to the "bathroom." The room had only a tub and a washbasin. Coming out, Ruth was rather confused, but our host said, "Oh, you meant the Loo." So we learned.

❋ You Said What?

There was a public park where on a Sunday afternoon anyone could take a soapbox, take a deep breath, and speak his or her thoughts, hoping to gather a crowd. Ruth saw this as an opportunity and in full voice said she had something that was out there to seduce the world: CocaCola. This subject gathered a few and this handful seemed to indicate that the subject had little appeal.

She switched then to taking off her glove, making it tremble and shake. She did some world-class shrieking. Ruth explained to the good-sized crowd that it was demons that were the cause of all this movement. She then stopped and almost whispered. All this time I was moving to the back of the crowd with my head low. She quietly informed all, that only money placed in the glove, would ever placate the demons.

So help me, she got a few coins. My guess is some folk do not want to even take a chance and took out demon insurance for a coin or two.

❋ Hold Your Breath!

The train trip south was about 70 miles to the work we were to do. It was at a church youth camp in a village called Wollongong. We were to build a cabin in the Youth Center for the Methodist Church. The trees had been cut a few years before, taken down with a menacing gas-driven lumber saw, as dangerous an item as I ever want to see for man or youth to operate. After a heavy safety lecture, we began to make boards out of trees. No plans, but the cabin began to take shape.

The group worked hard, so I soon divided them up into teams, with each team having time off to go into Sydney and be tourists. Trains servicing this community ran both local and express. Wollongong was on the local line. What happened next has the terror of making nightmares more vivid and valid.

South of the depot the two sets of rails made a curve coming toward the depot so that the approaching trains were hidden. The team got off of the local, and being teens, jumped down onto the tracks and crossed to the depot. They rejected the choice of taking the overhead crossing.

While they were in mid track, a fast Express train sounded its whistle coming around the blind curve. The boys ran and jumped up onto the depot platform. The girls also ran but, unable to jump, pressed their bodies to the depot platform wall next to the train track.

I was caught off guard when the police arrived, telling me that the express stopped a mile down the line and the engineer had thrown up, sick because of the carnage he was sure had just happened. More police came. So did a lot of railroad personnel. All left shaking their heads. Our teens had not owned up to what had just happened.

One girl lost one shoe. The saving issue was the express was going so fast it leaned out as it came around the curve, making room between platform and train that was there at no other time. Later I slid my hand down between the train and platform and my fist just loosely fit. Yes, the train was standing still. Yes, I have given thanks often for this which is for me a miracle, even as I do now. I chose not to relate this event to the parents when we got back home, as parents get upset easily by incidents like this.

❈ But It's Summer in California...

Ruth was the smart one and saved the day. While during the day it was mild temperature and we all enjoyed the kookaburra birds singing their song, it was still winter. In other words, it was bitter cold at night.

Being a guest of a family where we were invited to stay overnight, I was shown to my bed out on the screened porch. A thermometer registered 27 degrees; I hugged every blanket they provided me. It was no different at Wollongong.

Ruth took the train back to Sydney and returned with an armload of red rubber hot water bottles. Our excellent cook boiled water every night and filled the bottles. All was good. I do recall one girl who needed five of these to keep warm. The cook had one strange quirk, in that she feared spiders. Australia does have a wide variety of very deadly spiders. Ruth entered the kitchen and the cook was cowering in the corner. There was a large spider on the wall. Ruth took off her shoe, killed it, and the cook could not do enough for us from then on.

One of the villagers watched us work and when we had a break asked me to join him for a "bit of a puff." He meant to jog with him down to the "weer" and back, so thereafter I took time for a bit of a puff with a newfound friend. Wonderful people.

❈ The Studebaker

On the job, one of the girls fell and broke her arm. I got a car and quickly took her to the hospital in Sydney, but on the way, I saw an abandoned vintage car, with beautiful classic lines, sitting in a plowed field. It was love at first sight.

While the doctors were working on her arm, I went back and checked out this graceful auto of yesteryear. It was a 1924, 4 door Phaeton, right-hand drive, Dictator 6 Studebaker. Of course, the whole back end was rusted out, and the rest was repairable, but it had remnants of class.

I took the girl back to Wollongong, found the owner of the car, and bought it. Shipping anything across the ocean is expensive. I found a tramp steamer, and the price was right, but they were first going to Saudi Arabia to pick up some camels and drop them off in Japan. The camels ate the top and upholstery which I was going to use for patterns.

When it got to LA it had to go through a 30 day quarantine, having been so close to the camels. I restored it down to the frame and it took a blue ribbon, and best of show in a vintage car show. We had this classic in the family for 48 years before circumstances closed in on reality, and it was adopted by another family.

✳ Funny Stories

At a local church camp, the Aussies had us join them for a meal. They had an after-dinner entertainment custom. They would all start banging on the table and the noise would rise to a crescendo. In the quiet that followed, they would call out, "We want a funny story," from a named person. When I told my story I got a group response, a short laugh, then more banging, "We said we wanted a funny story."

At one of the churches we served, a member was the foreman of record production of Columbia Records. He would stop by every so often and drop off an armload of newest releases. I had little time to listen to the records but our eldest son was with us on this trip, and he had lots of time. One record was a comedian who did stand up adult humor.

He had memorized this adult comedian's whole act. Our son had no idea what was meant by all that he was saying but he sure had all of our mouths dropped open in attention. He got laughs at first, then it fell quiet as all realized what the comedian was really telling. The closing line was, "...take her home now, she's ready." We left ASAP.

Recently I asked him if he recalled doing this. He said he did, and he still had the record. You never know about the preacher's kid.

❋ Dr. Taylor

We had a bus for a week of sightseeing and first on my list was the capital of Australia, Canberra. At their war museum was the flight uniform of a WWI ace of aces, who was shot down behind Australian lines, Manfred Von Richtofen. This was "The Red Baron" who may have been the German fighter pilot who could possibly have been the one who shot down my associate pastor.

Why did I wish to visit his memorial? I had a retired missionary on my staff and he had flown in WWI and was shot down twice by "Von Richtofen Flying Circus'. I loved to get Dr. Taylor off of church business and talk about what it was like to be in an open cockpit fighter plane, testing his skills against the best. Dr.Taylor was our in-resident saint on the staff, and had been shot down twice, both times behind German lines. His stories of escaping kept my attention.

This incredible soul had, after the war, given his life as

a missionary in South America. I always felt he was God's gift to this church and to me. It was out of respect for the life of Dr. Taylor that I guided the team to this one bit of his life noted in a museum, the memorial to a German air ace with 80 kills to his credit.

✳ A Job Well Done

We saw and fell in love with the Australian people and their use of English. We had to learn such phrases as "Robot" for a traffic signal, "panel beater" for auto body work, "walkabout", etc. Making friends was easy. We were always welcome and befriended. They showed us the uniqueness of things, taking us with them on their walkabout. A friend led me to a barn filled with Model T Ford parts all laid out, in order for a buyer to order the body type and year T Ford someone wanted to buy. Then to a hangar housing a WWI Wasp fighter aircraft.

Asking about old cars, one person said there "is that thing in the attic."

I found a 1904 Oldsmobile sitting on sawhorses but not for sale. I offered everything I had including my socks, for it had been driven 15 miles, put in the attic, and the house completed. In other words, it was still brand new.

We had a rightfully earned sense of accomplishment of all we had done and seen as a team. No, the cabin we had worked on was not finished but anyone with a square and a hammer could put the finishing touches on what we had done. But it was the experiences of and with the Aussies that marked us all.

It was time to move along toward home, with a brief stopover in Samoa.

※ Magical Samoa

We landed in Western Samoa and I got a blunt first-hand lesson in what I did not know about geography. Having thought that American Samoa and Samoa were the same, I had made all arrangements with American Samoan, which was still some hours away by weekly boat. The Methodist Church in the nearby capital city of Pago Pago was called for help. I apologized to the church in America Samoa for not showing up and we stayed where we were.

These Samoans where we landed were not expecting us but they turned out to give us a hardy welcome, the men dressed in their dark blue Methodist Men jackets and white lava lavas. In hours, they arranged for a welcoming dinner to which people showed up with various kinds of food.

I threatened the team that if these wonderful people were treating us "drop-ins" so well, we would show our thanks by eating what they had brought. If anything moved they did not have to eat it, but try. If they were not hungry, to eat up anyway. The team turned to and outdid themselves and I was pleased they had done so well eating strange island food.

We left the table, and then to my surprise and chagrin, all of the men present took our places at the table. Then the women did the same when the men finished scraping up the scraps. Finally the children sat down to a few remaining crumbs. Few, if anyone, smiled at our cultural blunder, and I was red-faced embarrassed.

The next day a picnic was arranged at a village and I learned quickly that one does not rise above the head of the Chief, which is tricky when the Chief is sitting cross-legged on the ground watching all that was going on.

Things turned normal when a volleyball game was

organized. The play was intense until a rain squall came through. Team USA ran for cover. Samoans laughed and got soaking wet. Ten minutes later the rain stopped: they were all dry in minutes and the game went on.

✳ New Authority

A surprise that I was not prepared for was the change I received after my purchase. I was looking at a 1945 half dollar. Seems the WWII U.S. military stationed there left U.S. money. The Samoans had been passing it around ever since. I increased my old U.S. coin collection considerably.

Later I was made a Talking Chief by the Samoans, the kava bowl was filled with fermented something that all the men partook of as it was passed around. After which I was given a hand held authority symbol, a switch which I placed with my right hand over my left shoulder and this allowed me to speak with authority. I later learned this didn't work in Rotary meetings back home.

This also granted us a special place to sleep in the parsonage. Ruth was on an elevated bed covered with mosquito netting, and I was to sleep on the floor beside her. I soon climbed into bed with her under the net. We woke to the giggling of teenage girls, as this behavior was not proper.

At that time, the way one proposed marriage on Samoa was to sneak into an open hut and crawl in bed with the woman of choice. If she didn't scream, they were married. Unfortunately, the chief was looking for another wife -- so we were advised to keep our two fairest skin girls in the pastor's house - the only structure that had a lock.

The shower wasn't, in that it only dripped, and doubled as a urinal. That and a number of things needed fixing, so our team went to work to help where they could. Later, Ruth helped underwrite the remodeling with earnings from her first book published by Abingdon, "Underground Manual For Minister's Wives, etc."

About to leave for the US and home, we gave permission and watched as one team member called his parents, after which he informed us that he had an OK to stay in Samoa when the team left. To our embarrassment, his parents were waiting for him at LAX and asked us where their son was. We learned he had a fear of being drafted and took this way out...on a dead phone.

✳ The Samoan Thank You Dinner

As the custom was in Samoa, they traveled with one-way tickets. They came to our church to take a tour of churches with a show of dancing, fire swallowing, and Samoan food. The money given to them was to get them back home. With two vans from our church laymen and our son Mark's van, we helped take them on a church tour circuit.

As a thank you to the church, they put on a Samoan barbecue for the congregation. Two pigs were killed and cooked in a pit dug in our backyard. Lots of neighborhood kids watched until the pigs were butchered: suddenly the kids disappeared.

Cleaning up after the dinner, our Samoan friends innocently poured the fat from the pigs down the sink, plugging the church kitchen sinks solid.

For these and many other events, the Samoan venture remains in our minds, savored as a joyful time and memory.

The Kava bowl from which we all drank and my authority switch is here with us now.

✳ A Wedding Unlike Any

Arriving back home I found being a talking chief had its state-side obligations. We were invited to a wedding with a high learning curve. As expected we were seated at the head table with the couple and parents, as one of the places of honor. We knew no one and smiled a lot.

After the wedding ceremony concluded and well wish speeches were spoken, we were presented each with a whole roasted chicken. This quickly happened. Every guest got one chicken and no one seemed surprised. Following came a number of other dishes I have now forgotten, but there was applause as the food kept appearing. I was a bit bewildered, lost, and looking around, saw everyone opening sacks and putting all the gastritis treats in the bags they had brought. They did keep aside what they would normally eat at a feast, which indicated why the young men played lineman in college football. They realized we did not have anything to carry home this windfall, and two bags were soon provided and filled.

The father of the bride was at the door on our way out of the hall and I noticed that he was being slipped money to cover the cost of the wedding extravaganza in food,and we all left with a smile and avoided the weighing scale for several weeks.

We had a great time in Australia and Samoa, a host of memories, but we were awfully glad to be home and back to work as a parish pastor. And with it all, an inward smile recalling all that God had added to our lives, so much that was priceless.

✳ Mystery Guests

A number of years passed after we got home, and then a mystery appeared at our front door. It was a couple, greeting us like old friends. They had their luggage and said they would like to stay a week or so. Ruth and I assumed the other had extended such an invitation to them when we were Down Under. Their accent, his soft as a cloud hands, we knew he had sheared sheep and the lanolin always did make the shearer's hands soft.

Neither of us had any memory of them but we had new Aussie friends from Down Under, with no memory of meeting them before opening our front door. We never heard from them again.

TRIP NUMBER FOUR:

ITALY

❋ The Continent

It was happening again.

We had a call for a work team to go to an orphanage, in Italy located near Naples, and it was Methodist. Gathering teenagers willing to go was no problem. Leaving LAX in the evening and seeing the sunrise four hours later is always a wonder. We landed and one hour later we were off to "the city of lights", Paris and all of its tingling expectations.

Then all collapsed in a Youth Hostel, but being young, it was not for very long. The only one to volunteer (under pressure) to go with me to explore was our youngest son. We climbed to the roof of Notre Dame Cathedral and found the roofing was lead. Inside of this awesome structure was unbelievable stained glass, that makes you spit out your gum and drop to your knees. I did kneel at the grave of one of my heroes, Blaise Pascal.

Later we stumbled into a room that had scale models of castles in France and found the door to the back way to Napoleon's tomb. Got the team up and we climbed the numerous steps to Sacre Coeur for the view. The group split and did the tourist thing, seeing as much as possible on the run, which should be criminal or at least shameful to do inside The Louvre.

We left Paris on a bus and the noisy excited sharing of all they had seen and experienced, but now we were headed through some beautiful countryside on our way to Switzerland. This began the way to the unforgettable Alps. The next day being Sunday, we all went to a Methodist Church which was five floors underground. The team was asked to sing Amazing Grace and Ruth did a solo.

✳ Bucket List Skiing

On our tour through Europe we took a clogg railroad train to the Jungfrau Glacier where at the top you can see Spain, Germany, and France. I got to ski and was offered a job as a ski instructor. My creds went up with the team. We moved on to Interlaken and this is where on a high bridge Ruth called out, "O look, there is a pink elephant," and the whole team was at the windows looking, and a few swore they also saw it. Fatigue does that.

We all did see the enchanting charm of Grainau in the German Alps which holds the Passion Play every ten years. This was for their escaping the black death in 1633. Here our youngest son Nathan celebrated his 12th birthday. We shopped with the team, and still display and treasure the incredible basswood carvings they made which we procured.

It was Salzburg that had everyone talking about the film, "The Sound of Music," and there was a scramble to see it all. I felt I would be lynched if I got in the way.

Along with the dark and dinner time, I asked about our twelve year old son. Yes, he was with this group or seen in that place,or with that one of the team, but not lately. No panic, but do a quick walk looking for him. Then those who were concerned were divided and sent searching into the four quarters of the city. All found nothing. It was quite late and I was trying to control my fears. I was about to call the police when someone called out that Nate was in his bed fast asleep. Two strong emotions followed, first immense relief, and the other one came with a lecture.

Back in the bus one tripper wrote, "We were overcome by the beauty of the country, the forests, and meadows that would make a fantastic set for Little Red Riding Hood and Robin Hood." It was here we stopped and in a meadow had our church service. The liturgy was all of us giving thanks for such created splendor surrounding us in all we had and could see.

✳ Casa Materna

Taking a train for our goal of Napoli we arrived at 5:00 a.m. We stuck Ruth with all the luggage which beyond filled a taxi, and sent her on to Casa Materna on the outskirts of Naples.

Now to get the team there we had to identify the right bus. None of us could read any sign. Maybe it was an angel in disguise, but a small lad kept nodding his head and pointing to a bus number as we said, Casa Materna. After a while the right numbered bus did come along but was packed (read compressed) with locals. We thought the bus was jammed full but more got on at each stop.

I was mashed and unable to move and in mid bus. At a stop, one of the team stepped off to let a few locals decompress and depart. Before he could get back on, the door closed. From where I was, I yelled "STAY THERE."

This yell was reinforced by many but with a strong Italian accent.

At the next stop, unable to move, I yelled as loud as I was able to any team member by the door, to exit and stay glued there. This was done at nine stops with a hasty prayer, "Lord, please protect these kids." Arriving at Casa Materna, I jumped out, and running back along the bus route, I collected the team. Each one was on a corner, anxious but unharmed, thank God!

At the Casa, Papa Santi called all of us together, and welcomed the team, and thanked us for coming. I was thankful the team all got there. While I had heard that where we were going was the armpit of Naples, we found the Casa was housed on the edge of the Mediterranean Sea in a 200-year-old mansion once owned by a Prince, and a great place to be. We were glad to finally be here and it wasn't a hardship place to be as I had feared.

Our assignment was to fix whatever needed fixing. Our primary contribution was to relate to the orphans, mainly to love them and befriend them as much as possible. We soon found that their one goal was to challenge us to a soccer game. This was seriously said and I had a sudden feeling we were way out of our league. With that being my only real concern, we were shown to our rooms, and "crashed".

The surprise of the unimagined was when we were awakened by the orphanage band trying to play an unfamiliar tune: "My Country 'Tis Of Thee." There were moments the tune was recognizable. After a continental breakfast of a hard roll we went to morning worship. First, we all sang, and then Pastor Santi spoke on the conversion of Paul. This was in Italian of course, and I didn't understand a word, and I didn't wake any sleeping team member.

By 10:30 every one was wide awake and in the water, or on the beach. It may have been a black volcanic ash beach, but what a beginning. Afterward, we were led on a twenty-minute walk that took us an hour. We were now viewing the ruins of Porta Ercolano, like Pompeii, only it had been covered with mud, not ash.

That evening the guys played soccer and lost 6 to 2. I was politely told to stay on the bench (leave the game) as the orphans were putting the ball between and around my legs and giggling, having a grand time while doing it while chanting Italy six, America two. No one called the newspapers about this international soccer game.

The next day was a workday. After breakfast and worship, the girls handled cleaning classrooms, and the guys did yard work and repair. After lunch and a short siesta, all turned to the task of cleaning classrooms. The next day was given to sanding, painting, cleaning metal bedsteads, desks, and fixing holes in the roof and putting up shelves. Papa Santi, grateful for all that we accomplished, made the Casa bus available.

✳ The Buried City

The place to see on our day off, voted number one, was Pompeii. We saw the excavated ruts of the chariots worn into the pavement, which are the same width as US railroad rails. There were steam rooms, open highly decorated dining rooms, restrooms, and open parks. No end to the planning of this city.

My unspoken thoughts were of the year 70-71 A.D. Every Jew was taken prisoner and became slaves who lived following the bloodshed brought by Rome in the Holy Land, and the end of the nation of Israel. As Mt.

Vesuvius erupted in 79 a.d. and covered Pompeii in ash, I wondered how many Jews no longer were considered people but were under the lash of Roman slavery, serving their owners here in this city frozen in time. I counted the brothels, never pointed them out, but wondered if the granddaughters of the high priests were taken as slaves to serve here.

One never forgets the bodies now in plaster as the mortals that inhabited these forms faced the tragedy that took their lives. There was thoughtful reflection mixed with the noisy, shared discovery going back to the Casa.

We did take a trip later to climb Mt. Vesuvius. I picked up a piece of orange obsidian that I never knew came in that color. It now rests on our back porch and is still uniquely orange.

❊ No Blue Grotto For Us

Our artistic daughter saw a big wall in the boys dorm as a canvas. She got a ladder and started sketching on the wall, Peter Pan in flight over a ship. It was mural art, floor to ceiling. She was well into the mural when the team voted to take a day off and go to the Isle of Capri. All went except Becky and Ruth. They both stayed at the Casa and Ruth added the palm trees while Becky painted Peter Pan.

This was an out and out fun experience for the team. It is a tourist must-see,but because of the tight budget I never mentioned such things as The Blue Grotto, boat excursion, etc. Also, no comment on the perverted Emperor who ruled the vast empire from this place, who mentally was sexually twisted in his sick mind.

We walked, looked, and went back joy-filled and tired. Becky and her mother had accomplished a lot and I felt we had also. We found no water when we returned, even for the fifteen "johns" in the boy's dorm which flushed every time a train went by and shook the building. We all went to bed dirty and hoped for water in the morning.

We woke up to band music playing a rendition we all recognized as our national anthem. Tap water was available on and off all day. The orphanage kids did skits for us, all marking the joyous end of summer school. Everything was in Italian but we recognized "Zorba The Greek" and maybe "Santa Lucia." We were told they danced the "Hora" for us. It was loud and great fun, excitement running into high decibel numbers offered by all. (Read loud approval to all voice noise).

Following lunch, there was no water again to even wash our hands. Suddenly, the splash of water sounded and a rush to get toothbrushes, shampoo, or just soap. This time the water stayed on.

※ Wedding with a Sermon

Then an Italian wedding happened in the chapel. A couple who had worked at the Casa was tying the knot. They had not invited the American team dressed in T-shirts and Levis.The girls mostly did take it all in from any place they could, without being obvious.

First noticed was that the couple sat in chairs for a rather lengthy exhortation by Papa Santi. I was invited to the reception wearing a coat and tie.

But not the team; they ate the standard lunch in the mess hall. Then at bedtime one of the girls owned up to short sheeting all of the boy's beds. Becky was blamed for this and while most of us were at worship, Ron straightened all of Becky's clothes hangers and tied her shoelaces in knots. No boy suspected the shy quiet one of doing such a dastardly deed.

The next Sunday the surprise shock for us was that all the girls wore skirts. It gave a reason for respectful hand clapping. Breakfast was the same including a one hard bread roll. I didn't eat mine. I wrapped it and took it home and varnished it. It had a special place on my office bookshelf to remind me that there are places glad to have a small bit of bread once a day, no seconds, and sometimes no firsts.

※ Rome on Foot

Leaving, we piled into the Casa bus and said our goodbyes, which took 20 minutes and an unknown number of hugs. We did finally leave and in ten minutes were stopped cold in an impenetrable traffic jam. We just made it to the train on time, boarded, took our seats according to past tradition, and then found we were on the wrong train. The luggage was out the windows and into the windows of the right train, like the pros we were by this time on the trip. We mumbled apologies to those sitting in the seats on the other side of the train windows, with laps filled with our luggage.

Next was Rome where we earned this day the name Truman Tribe Trompers as the budget to see Rome was loud and clear; you walk. It was a zig zagging course as we took in what tourists had to see "riding on shank's mare," even if a bus ride was only 50 lira.

We paused at the Colosseum and in our mind's eye saw the gladiators, and heard the imagined roar of the 80,000 strong crowd. After that came the Forum, and numerous ancient places of power, making Rome the force it was.

The high point was St. Peter's Basilica and Vatican City. The crescendo was the awesome Sistine Chapel. All of this you have seen or need to see for yourself. A must for your bucket list.

I caused an uproar in a bank trying to cash in Austrian Shilling banknotes. No one in the bank knew what they were. All of the bank employees gathered shouting, joined by the bank president with a guard carrying a machine gun. You have to know what an Italian screaming match is, to understand the authority of a machine gun.

I won, got the money exchanged to the US coin of the realm and the team was solvent again. We were on our way home but just enough time to see the Fountains of Tivoli. The team exclaimed WOW with expectation of soon being in their own beds.

✳ Making Our Way Home

We moved on to Venice, the city of canals, and St. Mark's Cathedral. Crossing the Main Canal, we found the youth hostel built in the middle ages.

This is where my memory failed me. Our daughter called me on my error and since she was on this trip, who am I to dispute her? I had remembered very clearly that it was on the way home from Israel; not so. It happened on this trip on the way home. Being stubborn, I got out the letters the team wrote home to let the parents in on what was happening along the way. I was without question dead wrong. Here is what they wrote.

"At about 6:10 a.m., our group slowly stumbled to the ground floor of our Venice hostel, only to realize we were locked in! With the knowledge that we would never catch the train to Genoa if we waited for the management, Rev

Lee quickly came to a decision, then went to work with his small pocket knife. With his expert knowledge at work, we were soon outside, free from the locked doors. (We don't know where he learned this?)"

The water taxi was slow, making us miss the overnight sleeping compartment reservations we had for Paris, and without reservations on the next train, we stood up all night.

The team had to be at the Paris airport and do the paperwork. Tripper Melanie and I had gone on ahead to weigh in the luggage and found there was no need.

Arriving In London, we discovered that our baggage was not checked through to LAX, so Dave and I dug it all out of the plane's innards so the destination tags could be changed.

We landed in LA at 1:00 a.m. and it will take months for the team to tell all that was a part of this adventure, with the memory of the orphans still causing a smile.

We had experienced five different languages, odd customs, cold showers, strange food, feather beds, hard pillows, mosquitoes, subways, mountains and valleys, noise, filth, ruins, museums, youth hostels, and trains that we will never forget. We climbed a thousand steps, walked untold miles, and shopped in every kind of store. The girls had been pinched, honked at, and flirted with by professionals.

We parted as only close friends do and have all learned that America is still the best there is to live in, and we are thankful we do. But each of us came home different than we were when we left. Especially we thanked the parents who trusted to us the lives of those most dear to them, who tagged along via mail sent back home to share in their offspring's discoveries, experiences, and gilded edge memories.

TRIP NUMBER FIVE:

INDIA

We looked really good when we left

※ **Namaste**

I was chosen by my Rotary Club to take a "Group Study Exchange" to India, made up of four very bright young businesswomen. On second thought, they decided it would be wise if my wife was also added to the team. So, thank the Lord, from whom all gifts come, Ruth got to go along with me.

The whole trip was intense, fatiguing, exciting, and

overwhelmed with scenery. This included illnesses of many varieties which we had little or no defense against, so a few of us tried out as many as we could.

Our Rotary Club India host had planned every minute which meant that they wanted us to meet as many Rotarians in as many Rotary Clubs as possible. This meant that on a few days it seemed we met a different club about every 20 minutes. All clubs served the same special holiday food. We quickly learned to take a plate, smear some food on it, smile big, and then honestly say, "We have taken."

It was fatiguing. Every night a different host family bedded us down, all pleased to do what they could to make us comfortable and welcome. One night we were the guests of a delightful lady who was the head of a university chemistry department, and a climber of Everest. She gave up her bed for us, which was several 2" x 12"s with a sheet over the planks on sawhorses. Each member of the team had a different story every morning to tell, as did we, and it was always unique.

Then back into the minibus, in which we were being moved about, checking off places to go on that day's list. By team vote, we were sure our means of transportation had no springs and the frame was welded to something that found every pothole in the road. There was no dissenting vote.

The scenery overload was the noise, the smells, people pushing to get through the surging mass of humanity, and always the sacred cows to stumble over. I will leave this up to you to imagine an elephant-back tour looking for tigers with a rifleman at our backs for protection.

One day I answered a knock at the door and was greeted by two totally naked suntanned men. We sat down and talked 'til I figured out what god they were serving. I drew them into the conversation, noting they were both in their mid-thirties. I also found one had been a bank teller before this devotion to his god, that sent them begging for food. They each carried a tri-forked stick and were hungry, and we shared what we had.

In the foothills of the Himalayas, look any which way, and the view is picture-postcard awesome. Of course, when doing so is when you stumble over a sacred cow or step in some cow exhaust that has not been plastered on a wall to dry in order to cook our evening meal.

Events blur, but certain ones stand out. I was interested in their education system and visiting a school run by British nuns. A father with tears implored me almost on his knees, to speak a word to the nuns to let his daughter in the school. The problem was she could speak excellent English but was not so good in Hindi... And if the nuns were to keep their license this was a regulation: Hindi is the national language. To get a job, Hindi counts.

I asked the teachers in another school how they handled discipline. They pointed to a boy not learning up to his ability. He was, for that week, picking up papers and trash. He was told he would be doing that for the rest of his life if he didn't get an education. I heard he was soon back at his desk.

An acquaintance from the U.S. wrote to his father in India to find him a wife. His dad advertised in several newspapers and got a bundle of responses, which he then narrowed down to ten top runners and sent for his son to come and check them out. The son flew back to India, and interviewed all ten, asking each to fill out a questionnaire. The winner and finalist filled out his paper, then she handed *him* a paper of questions for him to fill out. They were joyfully happy in their marriage and a joy to have as friends.

Asking one Police Captain's quite attractive daughter about dating, she said she didn't date, explaining that her dad would make a better choice than she would or could.

As a pastor, I always checked as I could in premarital counseling if a couple really knew each other, and at times they didn't. Showing this to them was a skill I learned over time. Using cards of agree and disagree cards, it soon would be obvious they did not know each other. I also used the Johnson Temperament Personality test. Doing this was only once in a while.

Being a guest, you did not complain, only appreciated. A private bedroom was always a special gift for us to receive and escape India for a few hours. But a room with a shower had its own special meaning.

First, a servant came with a bucket of hot water. When he left we stood in a tub and poured the water over each other. Using a towel I rated somewhere on the industrial sandpaper scale, we dried off. Then the lights went off as electricity is diverted to area agriculture water pumps. The room was pitch black and we dressed by brail, leading to strange combinations of clothing in daylight.

A cup of steaming tea and something good to eat and the day had begun, knowing we were treated with the best they had and we were grateful.

✳ Visiting the People

I was invited to speak in a high school class. First I found a camped lineup on the outside of the school with mothers waiting for the next opening for registering. This was in the hope of their daughters being admitted to the school. The next bit was they did not mix the sexes and this school was all girls in their teens in this place of learning. They told us: "We found mixing sexes was a distraction."

As expected, the courtyard was filled with a giggle of girls, about two hundred as an estimate.The bell rang and they were quickly in their seats, three to a desk. When we walked in they quietly stood. The teacher said something in Hindi, and never raised her voice. She had them sit, and then introduced me to the class in English. I spoke and never lifted my voice. They put up their hands to ask a question but always with the greatest respect. This is truly a world away from the film "Blackboard Jungle."

The poverty was beyond description; we found that there were those who rented spots on the sidewalk, outlined in chalk, for a place to sleep. This made us very aware that we were being looked after by what seemed to be the new middle class.

I walked before dawn with a businessman who had a small place where they were making propane stoves for cooking in the home, replacing dried cow dung as fuel. I enjoyed the fellowship, but his reason to walk so early was his belief that early dawn's first light washed his eyes clean. My jolt, strolling with him, was seeing a US tank mounted on a pedestal with the sign announcing the tank was taken in battle with Pakistan.

The royal rich also had us as house guests. The top of this list was the owner of Modi Tire Ltd. It was grandeur beyond reality. A park-like setting with high walls surrounded this magnificent spot, but it had slums on all sides. I counted twenty-nine house servants. There was also a walled community for Modi employees that was clean and orderly, with its own TV station. It had 24-hour broadcasting with constant advertising under anything shown. His factory had huge signs such as

"Work Is To Worship," etc. I remembered I saw at least 200 or more men sitting hand-breaking rocks into gravel. Having worked on a rock crusher this was crazy. Asking their boss he quietly said "and what would these men do to feed their family?"

I recall in our conversation that Mr. Modi spoke of his concern about the problems India had, and his ideas to deal with what he saw as fixable, commenting that maybe he needed to enter politics. As of this writing, Narendra Modi is the Prime Minister of India.

✳ A Wedding, India Style

We were invited to a wedding but did not realize it was a five day affair. There was a canvas hung from the corners of four buildings covering the intersection of two streets which were now closed. They had what could only be called a throne that the bride and groom intermittently occupied. The bride was to keep her head down out of modesty, but with her glances she sure was keeping track of all things happening. Our team women were inundated with requests to dance. I received several mouthed requests: "Rescue me." There was music that was painfully loud, played continuously for two nights, and we excused ourselves with ringing in our ears, since two nights were enough to consider they were husband and wife, but with possible hearing problems.

✳ If it Sounds Unbelievable...

Our hosts without exception prepared food for the team, not like that prepared for their Indian guests. Our set apart fare would not sear the rust off of a rusty steel bar. Often we would see the food being prepared in the driveway over burning used munchies provided by cows. Our food was always separate and you only made the mistake of partaking of the wrong dish once.

We encountered several of the Overseers of small kingdoms, often referred to as Raja, which seemed to mean some kind of royalty. One such took me out to what could be called a garage. I was shown what I recall was a Vauxhall, in pristine shape, and shown with the polish of a showroom sales floor. One caregiver had the daily job of it's upkeep. I was told it had not run in ten or more years.

In India if it sounds unbelievable, it is most likely true. Illustration: we looked in on a temple overrun (meaning beyond numbers) by big fat rats. People were bringing food for the rats, when a few bringers looked like they needed the calories on their own plates. It was the belief that the rats were their reincarnated ancestors. I have in confidence heard this about lawyers and even mothers-in-law, but never envisioned their now being live rats. This was the real thing.

Try this for a different way to do things: In case of an auto accident no vehicle was moved till the case was settled in court, which often took months. Traffic just went around the wrecks by turning out into the field and going on its way.

A one-oxen cart was in the center of the road plodding along. Asking our driver for an explanation, I was told the cart had a license and the owner had the right.

The team fitting into India culture,
with a lot of fun pretending

✻ India's Final Gift

The women on our team were all taller than the average person in India, and they were stared at as something to behold, especially the team members who had blond hair. We were told that some had walked miles to sit and stare at this rare sight. The two blondes, the tiny one from Texas, and the 5'8" one were visibly stared at by the people in the crowds that followed us everywhere. A Rotary team from Ohio of young businessmen who traveled with us, got much less attention than did our women.

A silo of stories is stored up about what came out of this team experience. In the fourth week, the Indian sickness hit us. I regret that I was half sick and half afraid to leave the team and go by myself to see Sister Teresa and her work while she was alive. I admired her dedication and still treasure her books.

Back in the states, members of the Indian church we

were nesting, had made arrangements for me to speak to the Christians in India in the area they had migrated from. Word reached me that a massive number of people had gathered, of all faiths. I regret that I had to back out because I had a serious case of "the trots."

One of our team members was so ill that she thought she would die. One of the team was down and asked for chicken soup, which her host family provided, but with the whispered request that she would tell no one that they ever provided this soup as they were Hindus. When back in the states, after a long period of sickness, she had to have her thyroid gland removed.

On the next and last week's agenda was a visit to a car assembly plant that Mr. Modi had arranged for us that they were excited for us to take. The team voted to forgo the visit to the manufacturing car plant, then they all voted to wimp out and come home a week early, ending the trip at LAX. So ended our inside view of India.

Going through customs at LAX with a good idea why my wife was so long in "the loo", was what we all had as a gift from India. With understanding this, I patiently waited. When she exited sometime later, all of the officials had vacated their stations, so she never went through customs. Happy wife, happy life.

I did ask her if she ever wanted to return to India and her answer was yes, but she went on to add these conditions: "If we stayed at the Hyatt Hotel, ate at the Hyatt Hotel, and traveled in a sealed Hyatt Hotel bus." That was very clear and we have never returned to India.

✳ The Travel Epilogue

After laying aside my clerical life, we couldn't stop using this form of seeing our wide world. In 2000, we took an adult group to Oberammergau to experience the Passion Play, but avoided youth hostels in any form, or sitting on the curb to eat our dinner or going steerage on shipboard. Not nearly as much fun but way more comfortable.

Then came the cruise ships: three times on the Mediterranean, a notable cruise around the Horn on which our daughter-in-law's father died, the self guided rivers of France on a barge and the Russian Rivers from Moscow to Petersburg.

We arrived in Moscow on September 11, 2001. Our Russian host informed us that the Twin Towers in New York City had been hit, along with The Pentagon, and a plane had crashed in the fields of Pennsylvania. I was in Moscow, and I was sure we had landed at the start and dead center of WWIII. Instead, and much to our surprise, the lovely Russian people offered us their condolences and the American Embassy had flowers in front, shoulder high.

Home looked especially good after that trip.

✳ Blessed

Now retired for 25 years, we have been blessed to see so much of our world and to know that Christians are everywhere. We sang, we prayed and worshipped in so many situations, in so many countries, and praised God for such amazing opportunities.

Ruth and I cherish the memories of so many people and cultures. It is our prayer that wherever we have gone, we have brought the spirit of Christ with us. Because our life has taken us from total poverty to comfortable retirement, we can only say,

What a life! Thank you, Lord, thank you for guiding us every step of life's way.

Ruth and Lee

Rev. W. Lee Truman, B.A., M.Div., Ph.D.
M. Ruth Truman, B.S., M.S.,Ph.D,
Memory Checker, Editor
Rebecca Joy Truman, B.A., Editor
Carlson Aba, B.S., Computer Consultant